W9-AUC-253

6/00

the Weekend Crafter

Woodburning

the
Weekend
Crafter

Woodburning

20 Great-Looking Projects to Decorate in a Weekend

BETTY AUTH

LARK
BOOKS

ASHEVILLE, NORTH CAROLINA

EDITOR:
KATHERINE M. DUNCAN

ART DIRECTOR & PRODUCTION:
KATHLEEN J. HOLMES

ADDITIONAL PHOTOGRAPHY STYLING:
THOM GAINES

PHOTOGRAPHY:
EVAN BRACKEN

ILLUSTRATIONS:
ORRIN LUNDGREN

PRODUCTION ASSISTANCE:
HANNES CHAREN

This book is dedicated to my husband John—
thanks for everything.

Library of Congress Cataloging-in-Publication Data
Available
Auth, Betty.
    Wood burning : 20 great-looking projects to decorate in a weekend /
Betty Auth.
        p.   cm.— (The weekend crafter)
    Includes index.
        ISBN

10 9 8 7 6 5 4 3 2 1

First Edition

Published by Lark Books
50 College St.
Asheville, NC 28801, US

© 1999 by Betty Auth

For information about distribution in the U.S., Canada, the U.K.,
Europe, and Asia, call Lark books at 828-253-0467.

Distributed in Australia by Capricorn Link (Australia) Pty Ltd., P.O. Box
6651, Baulkham Hills Business Centre, NSW 2153, Australia

Distributed in New Zealand by Southern Publishers Group, 22
Burleigh St., Grafton, Auckland, NZ

Printed in China by L.Rex Printing Co. Ltd.

ISBN

CONTENTS

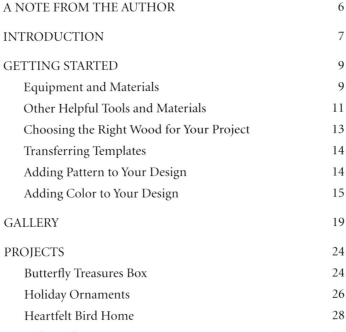

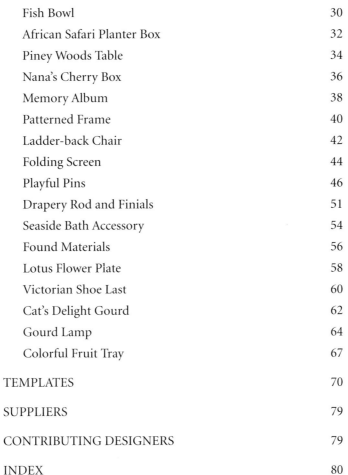

A NOTE FROM THE AUTHOR

In the year 2006, it will be a hundred years since my grandmother, Florence, created a lovely, woodburned box. She was single and away from home for the first time while attending business school. Photographs of her in 1906 show a pretty, young girl wearing a white blouse with a high, ruffled collar and a cameo brooch. Her light brown hair is pulled up in a Gibson Girl hairdo. The first automobiles were just becoming available, and Victorian manners ruled the day.

My grandmother's cherry box along with pieces that I created years later

Florence apparently learned to woodburn as an inexpensive way to make gifts for her loved ones and "while away" the hours after her studies were done. Eighty years later, my mother Lucille passed the box on to me. Mom always kept it in the drawer of her nightstand, and put her watch and earrings there before going to bed. Mom wasn't a very sentimental soul, and few material things held meaning for her, especially if they were old. She was always looking for the newest, latest, and most modern of things, and gave away anything that had been hanging around for too long. Because she kept it close to her, I know that the woodburned box that her mother made really meant a lot to her, as it does to me now.

As the artistic one in the family, I'm always looking for ways to express my creativity. Woodburning is about the best way that I've found to make beautiful objects that will last through time. Perhaps my daughters, Terri and Valerie, will become interested in burning designs on wood. Or maybe my granddaughter, Amberly, will carry this art form into the next century, and make some beautiful things for her children.

This is a craft that everyone in the family can do, including kids and dads. It's my hope that you'll become intrigued with the possibilities that you find here and begin creating your own precious treasures to pass down through your family.

Betty Auth

My grandmother, Florence Dorsey, at a young age

Woodburning set made for children, 1953. Collection of Betty Auth

Pamplets explaining how to do pyrography were used during the Victorian period when elaborate designs were popular.

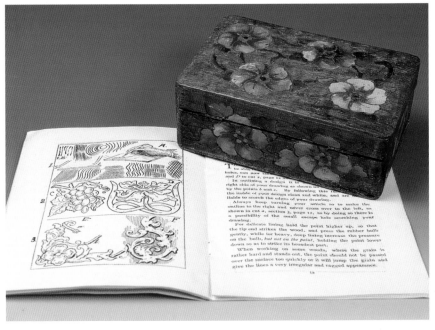

Over the course of your life, you've probably seen examples of woodburned designs and never thought about how they were created. If you have done woodburning in the past, it may have been as a Girl or Boy Scout.

Perhaps you own woodburned heirlooms made by a Victorian grandmother, such as a box or chest filled with sentimental keepsakes or a cheerful plaque burned with a pithy saying. These objects are decorated with incised designs that resemble drawing, using an art that has been called by many names: woodburning, burnt wood, "pyrography", "pokerwork," and "Flemish Art." Versions of this craft can be found worldwide where woodburning has been used to decorate everything from simple wooden spoons and breadboards to intricate boxes, vases, cabinets, and furniture.

In America, woodburning reached its heyday during the Victorian era when improved tools and equipment made wood-burning accessible to almost anyone, and supplies were sold through mail-order catalogs. Thousands of wooden boxes, tables, shelves, and other items were prestamped with designs that fed the Victorian craving for creating decorative, ornate furnishings for their homes.

Before the Victorians adopted this craft, it was simply called pokerwork. Pokers and other metal tools were heated in a fireplace or furnace before using them to burn designs in wood. Anyone who did this had to heat several pokers in the coals at the same time so that a hot one was always available to continue burning the design. The intense heat and inevitable accidents of working in front of a fire made it a less-than-perfect craft.

When a platinum point was developed for woodburning at the end of the 19th century, much of the awkwardness of pokerwork was eliminated. The new point stayed hot longer since wood-burning sets came equipped with a small bottle of benzine which served as a portable heat source. The flame used to heat the tip of the woodburner was kept active by squeezing a small bellows by hand or pedaling one by foot. The temperature of the point could be controlled, and the results of burning became more predictable. Fine points allowed for the creation of more complicated designs. The Victorians claimed this art as their own, assigning it the lofty name of "pyrography" or "fire writing." At the turn of the 20th century, the Flemish Art Company was established in Chicago to supply the demand for

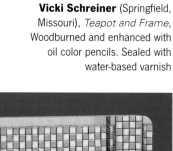

This Victorian dresser box may have been used to hold items such as hair combs. Collection of Betty Auth

wooden items to burn. Because of the thousands of pieces of raw wood which the company sold stamped and ready for burning with their tools, pyrography became known as "Flemish Art." The Flemish Art Company logo can still be found on the bottom of a variety of antique woodburned items.

A century later, woodburning in America is undergoing a rebirth. Today, woodburning ranges from handsome, simple designs that adorn useful items to complex, fine-lined drawings in wood. You can buy equipment and materials that provide sophisticated results with a minimal amount of fuss. First, designs are transferred to preformed wood pieces made of basswood, pine, or birch using a pattern, a rubber stamp, or stencil. After burning the designs with an easy-to-use woodburner shaped like a ballpoint pen, color is added with oil pencils, transparent blending gels, and stains.

Vicki Schreiner (Springfield, Missouri), *Teapot and Frame*, Woodburned and enhanced with oil color pencils. Sealed with water-based varnish

Through this book, you'll experience the instant gratification of burning designs on a variety of wooden forms in a few simple steps. Besides traditional forms such as boxes and plaques, you'll be amazed by the updated use of woodburning on forms that range from jewelry to furniture. Soon you'll be teaching your children and friends the tricks of the trade of this versatile and lasting art.

About the Projects in This Book

The projects in this book represent a variety of styles and possibilities for woodburning. Pick and choose the ones that you like, and explore the craft by following the simple steps provided. You'll be able to complete many of the projects in only a few hours, and others you'll be able to finish in a couple of days. Keep in mind that you can alter the projects that you see by simply applying a design to another form, repeating and combining designs, or making up your own. The gallery pages will inspire you for future projects. Once you begin this friendly craft, you'll see all kinds of possibilities for burning—from unfinished drawers to kitchen cabinet doors!

GETTING STARTED

In this chapter you'll find everything you need to know to begin woodburning, including explanations of equipment and techniques, as well as instructions for creating all the patterns and textures that are used later in the project section. You'll also learn about adding color to your woodburnings through wax-based oil pencils, transparent blending gels, and stains. Read this chapter before beginning the projects, and then refer back to it as needed for more detailed information on materials or techniques.

This chapter also explains the suitability of different woods for projects. Surface choice can be a crucial factor in the success of a woodburned piece, so pay attention to this information. Talk to a salesperson if you have questions about the wood you're buying at specialty wood shops, unfinished furniture stores, home supply stores, or a local lumberyard. Most of the unfinished wood pieces used in the projects for this book are premade out of a particular kind of wood and are available through the suppliers listed at the back of this book.

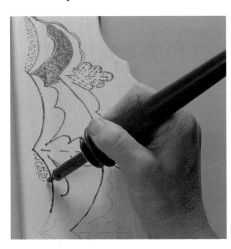

Equipment and Materials
WOODBURNERS

All of the projects in this book were created with a constant temperature, solid shaft electric woodburner that heats the tip, or point, to about 950°F. Suitable for both beginning and advanced levels of expertise, this woodburner is among the least expensive available and uses a small amount of electricity.

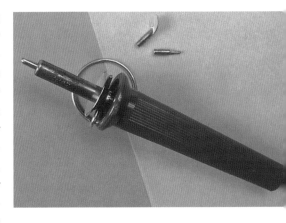

Several brands that are similar in their range of applications are available through mail-order catalogues or in craft and hobby stores (see suppliers' list on page 79).

When you buy a solid shaft woodburner, it comes equipped with a universal point, which was designed to perform all techniques without changing points. This point is similar to the wedge-shaped point that you may have used years ago as a child. Although this point can be used for many different techniques, it can be difficult for a beginning woodburner to master because it has a sharp tip that can gouge the wood, and the rigid wedge along its base makes it difficult to burn curved lines. We suggest that you put it aside for the time being, and purchase the three points discussed below: a small, rounded

In the early 1970s, Scott Ladd, who was associated with Walnut Hollow, became interested in woodburning. At that time, changing points was cumbersome because the solid shaft woodburner point was permanently affixed in the end of the woodburner's shaft. (An example of this vintage system is pictured on page 7.) To change points, you had to screw a second one over the permanent point. Because of the layers created by this process, the added point never heated sufficiently. To improve the system, Scott worked with metallurgists to modify a soldering iron so that the original point could be removed, and interchangeable replacement points screwed into the hollow shaft without losing the heat required for effective woodburning.

point, a large, rounded point, and a shading point. (If you decide to try a universal point, first sand the point and wedge so that they slide more easily over the surface).Using these points, you'll be able to switch from a very fine point to a broad shading point without interrupting the flow of work.

Using the Woodburner and Points

Never touch any part of the woodburner except the plastic handle. To begin burning a design, hold the woodburner by the handle like a pencil, but move the point with half the speed of one. (Because the handle is somewhat fatter than a pencil, it may take a few moments to get used to its width.) Hold the point at a normal writing angle

---

SAFETY TIPS

■ When the woodburner is hot, and you need to change points, use needle-nose pliers with rubber handles to carefully grasp its lower, wider portion before unscrewing the hot point and placing it on a glass, metal, or ceramic surface to cool. Then pick up a different point, position it carefully in the shaft, and screw it into place. Since the pliers are now hot, place them on the same heat-resistant surface as the points.

■ If you're using a woodburner with a child, supervise them in the process of removing the hot point, or do it for them.

■ Each woodburner comes with a bent wire holder for cradling the upper shaft of the burner, so that it doesn't touch the surface on which you're working. For convenience and safety, tape the holder to a ceramic tile or saucer before taping it to the worktable.

---

or higher with the awareness that the shaft is as hot as the point and will also burn the surface that it touches.

Due to the extreme heat of the point of a woodburner, the lightness or darkness of a design is controlled by the length of time that the point rests on the wood, not by the amount of pressure that you use. As long as the hot point is touching the surface, it will continue to burn. Because of this factor, lift the point from the surface at the beginning and end of a line to avoid spots and blurs. If the point begins to drag, or isn't making as dark a line as you desire, check for black carbon deposits. If the point is dirty, wipe it off lightly on a piece of sandpaper.

As you create the lines and shading of your design, keep turning the wood to reach different areas comfortably. To make a smooth, flowing line, pull the point toward yourself or across the wood, rather than pushing and causing it to dig into the wood.

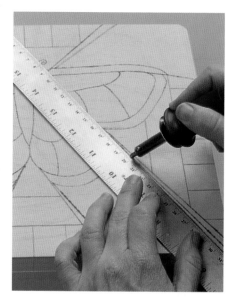

Because the brown lines burned in the wood are covered with miniscule flakes of ash deposited on the wood's surface, you'll need to brush or blow away the excess from time to time. Doing this assures that your design is burned deeply enough to remain after the ashes are wiped away.

There are various points available on the market, but you only need three to complete the projects in this book. The following versatile points provide the means to create different degrees of line detail and shading.

Small, Rounded Point

This point resembles that of a ballpoint pen and works well for burning details and patterns on soft woods such as basswood. Write or draw with this point as you normally do with a pen or pencil, but at a much slower pace. It's convenient to first use this point to draw lines of your design before accenting them with a large, rounded point.

To add stippling, or dots, hold either point perpendicular to the surface (straight up and down), touch the wood briefly to create the desired size of dot, and then lift. Holding the point on the surface longer will result in deeper, larger dots.

Large, Rounded Point

This point is a wider version of the small, rounded point, and the two are often used on the same areas of a design to create contrasting thicknesses of line. Use it to write and draw a thicker line when you need it. Choose this point if working on harder woods such as birch, as well as uneven or rough woods such as pine. It will produce a lighter, finer line on hardwoods such as oak or birch than it will on softwoods such as basswood.

Shading Point

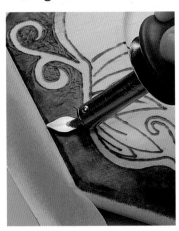

The shading point is a shovel-shaped point that is used for creating dark areas that make up backgrounds and other shaded areas of a design. It can also be used to make blended and feathered marks that look like shadows. To use it, hold the flattened part of the point level with the wood surface while moving it in small circles. You'll discover that it has a "sweet spot," similar to that of a golf club. Once you find the right angle, the point will burn the wood very quickly, so keep it moving at the same angle while you continue to burn the surface.

Wire Points and Rheostats

Some artists prefer using a controlled temperature woodburner that is equipped with a rheostat to adjust the heat of the point. These burners are usually equipped with interchangeable wire points that produce very finely detailed, controlled burning. This woodburning system is more expensive and difficult to use than a basic woodburner, which is more than adequate for a beginner. If you become proficient at woodburning, and want to be able to achieve highly detailed compositions in wood, a controlled temperature woodburner might be a good choice.

David A. Gregory (Eldrid, New York), *The Covered Bridge*, Woodburned basswood enhanced with colored oil pencils and stains

Other Helpful Tools and Materials

■ A tool you'll use often is a pair of needle-nose pliers. Be sure to buy a pair with rubber or plastic-covered handles so that you won't get burned when using them to remove the heated point on your woodburner before replacing it with another.

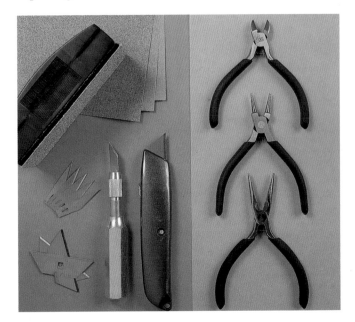

■ Often you'll need to sand a wooden surface before burning it to even out flaws and inconsistencies in the wood. You may also need to sand away old varnishes before burning treated wood. Overall, the process removes a top layer from the wood, and contributes to better, cleaner burned lines. Use a medium-grain sandpaper to smooth rough areas, and then finish off with a fine-grained sandpaper. Sanding blocks, which can be purchased at hardware or paint stores, are handy for finishing rough corners on boxes, planters, and other items.

■ If you need to cut a hole in a piece, particularly a gourd, a craft knife works well for gouging out a piece. Round off the edges with sandpaper after you've cut a hole.

■ A cork-backed metal ruler is helpful for burning straight lines because it doesn't slip while you're running the woodburning point along its edge. The 6-inch (15 cm) size is the most versatile.

■ A half gray and half white eraser from an office supply store is great for removing pencil and graphite paper lines from wood. The gray end contains grit that works like sandpaper, and the white end is smooth and colorless when used on wood. Emery boards and small bits of sandpaper are also helpful for erasing unwanted marks.

■ For reducing and enlarging designs, a proportional scale purchased at an office supply store is helpful. It is composed of two plastic circles marked with measurements and percentages. Locate the size of your original on the inner circle, then turn the circles until matched with the size that you want for your design. When you look inside the open window in the smaller circle, you'll see the percentage of reduction or enlargement required to create a design of that size. Set the photocopier to that percentage, and you'll have a correctly sized design.

■ Masking tape is handy for several jobs:
— To avoid knocking your heated woodburner onto the floor, tape the woodburner's wire holder to a ceramic tile or a saucer before taping both to the worktable.

— Tape paper templates to the wood to hold them in place over graphite paper while outlining designs on your wood surface (photo 1).

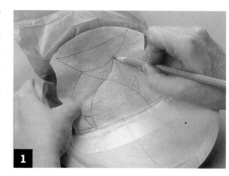

— Use two layers of masking tape to cover areas of the wood that you don't want to burn accidentally, such

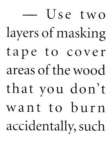

3

4

as inside corners where it's difficult to reach without burning the surrounding sides *(photo 2)*.

— Use tape to hold the edges of a box together while burning it *(photo 3)*.

— Mask off areas that you want to shield from staining *(photo 4)*.

Choosing the Right Wood for Your Project

In the United States, three primary types of unfinished wood—pine, birch, and basswood—are readily available and work well for woodburning projects. In other countries, different varieties may be found, or different names may be applied to these woods.

Most of the projects in this book use premade forms assembled out of pine, birch, or basswood that you can order from a catalogue or buy at a craft supply store. Each wood has its own characteristics that may make it more or less suitable for certain projects. The following information will assist you in making intelligent choices about the kind of wood to use with a particular project.

PINE

Pine is one of the least expensive of woods, and you'll be able to find premade pine forms in craft stores or discount chains. Because of its varied texture, it lends itself nicely to primitive, folk art designs. When you look at it, you'll notice graining, or darker streaks of color

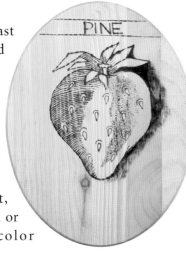

throughout the surface. These lines are harder and denser than the surrounding areas, and your point may skip over them before sinking slightly into the surrounding, softer areas. The best way to deal with the grain of pine is to work at a very slow pace using a large, rounded point. Don't use a lot of pressure, but allow the point to float over the surface as it was designed to do.

BIRCH

Birch is a strong, lightly colored wood with a smooth grain that burns evenly. Because of its hard surface, it burns lighter than softer woods. Burn birch slowly using a large, rounded point.

BASSWOOD

Basswood, a light, evenly grained wood, is by far the best choice for woodburning because it burns quickly and evenly. Even though it is slightly more expensive than other common woods on the market, it is well worth buying when you plan to invest a lot of time in a project.

PLYWOOD

Cabinet-grade plywood can be used effectively for hand-cut projects, such as the frame on the cover of this book. Choose a plywood that has at least a ¼-inch (.6 cm) ply. If you burn plywood with a thinner ply than this, you may burn through the top layer of wood to the adhesive layer and release noxious fumes.

ANTIQUES OR OLD WOOD

Before burning old or antique woods, it is essential to first remove all traces of varnish or other finish by sanding the areas to be burned. The antique shoe last project on pages 60-61 uses an old wood which has been thoroughly sanded before being burned.

If you find an antique, such as a box, that has a very heavy coat of old varnish that is problematic to remove, burn a design on a small, thin piece of basswood of a size that fits the lid, and attach it with wood glue, then allow it to dry overnight.

Transferring Templates

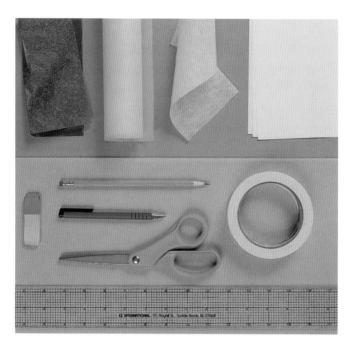

The designs used on the projects in this book are traced onto the wood with a template and graphite paper before burning them. After selecting a template, size the design to fit your wood surface. The simplest way to accomplish this is by enlarging or reducing it on a photocopy machine. You'll be able to trace the design from the photocopy paper, or you can transfer it to tracing paper, if you prefer a thinner paper. Cut out the design, leaving a border around it. Use masking tape to hold it in place along the top edge before slipping a piece of graphite paper underneath it, graphite side to the wood. Press firmly along the lines of the design with a pencil or ballpoint pen to transfer the design *(photo 5)*. As you work, it may be necessary to move the graphite paper around in order to trace all areas. When the tracing is complete, retrace any undefined lines with a pencil.

To transfer designs on curved portions of the wood, trace the designs onto non-fusible interfacing made for sewing purposes *(photo 6)*. (Never use fusible, iron-on interfacing for this purpose.) This cloth-like material is flexible and somewhat transparent, so it's easy to trace a pattern onto it. To do this, place a piece of interfacing over your design. Trace the pattern with a ballpoint pen instead of a pencil to prevent tearing. Next, cut the interfacing into manageable pieces. Slide each section into or over the contours of the curve that applies. Tape it into place, slide graphite paper underneath, and trace the lines of the template with a ballpoint pen *(photo 7)*.

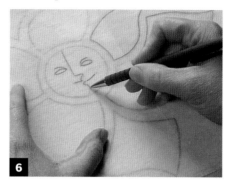

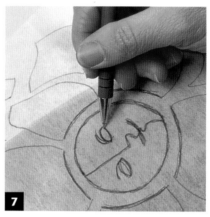

Adding Pattern to Your Design

There are a variety of ways to create woodburned patterns. The following examples will show you how you can use simple lines and dots to create a host of surface variations. Each pattern square pictured on page 15 is completed with a small, rounded point on the top half and a large, rounded point on the bottom, to show how thickness of line can affect the final look of the design.

1. *Zigzags:* This pattern is full of movement. To create it, touch the point to the wood, and move it back and forth in a "z" motion, without lifting the point from the surface. Keep adding lines parallel to one another. In this example, the lines are drawn straight across the wood, but you can also curve the lines of this pattern or make it circular. Pencil in guidelines to keep the pattern on track.

2. *Dashed lines:* This pattern works well for filling in a background or other area that needs to be slightly darker than the wood. Pencil in simple, parallel lines consisting of dashes before burning them to make this pattern. Curve the lines to create a dimensional appearance.

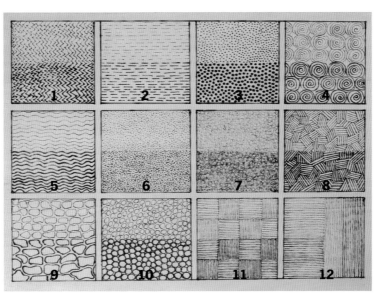

3. *Dots:* Randomly spaced dots will add life to your piece. To make this pattern, hold the woodburner point straight up, touch it to the surface, and leave it there until each dot is as dark as you want it. Keep the dots random without developing a pattern of rows. For fine shading, place the dots close together, and allow them to fade out or feather at the edge of the shaded area.

4. *Spirals:* Add interest to a design with a series of small or large snail-like spirals. Place them randomly or evenly in rows, as seen here. Pencil guidelines are helpful for creating this design.

5. *Wavy lines:* This soft, restful pattern is useful for covering large areas.

6. *Stippling:* This method of rapidly producing very small dots that are closely placed together is traditionally used in drawing to create soft shading and fill backgrounds of a design. Use a small, rounded point to quickly dot the surface of the wood in a staccato-like fashion.

7. *Scribbling:* For shading and other dark areas of a design, this technique is relatively quick and simple. Move the point in a continuous motion of small circles without lifting it from the wood. Overlap more of the same technique to darken areas further.

8. *Hatching:* This technique is composed of small sets of parallel lines laid down in varying directions. Use hatching to create texture or darken areas of a design. Allow the lines to fade out at the edges for a soft, shadowy look. To create what is known as cross-hatching, go back over the lines with another set laid down at right angles to the first.

9. *Snake skin:* This is an interesting pattern for lightly shading large areas of a background, or adding texture to an object. Repeat uneven, rounded, rectangular shapes adjacent to one another to cover an area. Place the shapes randomly or in straight lines, and size them differently to vary the design.

10. *Circles:* This pattern can be used to cover an unevenly shaped area, or to fill in a border or stripe in a design. Draw small circles of roughly the same size close together. Using the large, rounded point will produce dramatic, bold texture. Use pencil guidelines to confine the design where you want it.

11. *Basket weave:* This is an elegant, even pattern that can be adapted for large or small areas, or used as a border when at least two rows are used together. Draw evenly spaced pencil guidelines first, using a ruler if needed. Burn squares of parallel lines in one direction, then burn lines in the opposite direction.

12. *Parallel lines:* Create staight or curved parallel lines to add shading and depth to an area. Alter the distance between the lines and their density for variety.

Adding Color to Your Design

Two of the most popular mediums used to add color to woodburning are wax-based oil pencils and transparent blending gels. You'll see both used in the project section

of this book. Pencils and gels produce similar effects, are both easy to use, and are easy to correct if you make a mistake. When used sparingly, neither will obscure previously burned designs, and you'll be able to burn more designs right on top of them. Wood stains can also be used to add color to larger areas of a piece. The following section will introduce you to these mediums.

WAX-BASED OIL PENCILS

Wax-based oil pencils may seem familiar to you because they resemble the wax crayons that you used as a child. Artists have used them for years, and in the early 1970s, the Walnut Hollow company first marketed them for use on wood. These pencils consist of pigments in an oil and wax base that are encased in wooden shafts. They can be sharpened by hand or with an electric pencil sharpener.

Because they contain wax, oil pencils adhere well to wood. You can use them to color areas that range from soft, pastel colors to dark, solid colors, depending on the pressure that you exert when using them. They can be layered and blended to create a wide range of colors. Experiment with oil pencils on a scrap of wood before beginning. The following descriptions that correspond to the squares above them tell the effects that different amounts of pressure create:

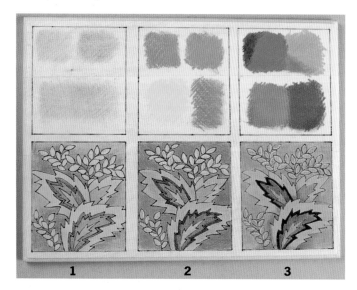

1   2   3

1. *Using light pressure to achieve a textural effect:* Lightly sketching layers of color that allow the wood to show through will lend areas a pastel, sketchy appearance, akin to watercolor paint. To do this, sharpen the pencil well, then hold it lightly. Lower the point to the surface, and allow it to skim the wood, moving it back and forth evenly as you cover areas. Turn the object and repeat this

light coverage from another direction. Continue until the desired depth of color is achieved.

2. *Using medium pressure for a variety of effects:* You'll produce more color by using more pressure. First, sharpen the pencil well and hold it as if you're writing. Bear down with the same pressure as you would on paper that has multiple copies attached. Cover the area with short back and forth or circular motions, allowing some of the wood's texture to show through.

3. *Using heavy pressure to achieve full color coverage:* For this technique, hold the pencil upright, and press as firmly as you can without breaking the point. Work the pencil back and forth in short strokes, being careful not to skip areas. This will produce the full depth of color possible with these pencils.

The following tips explain several ways that you can apply oil pencils to create different effects:

■ *Layering to create new colors:* Layer one color over another to create a third, blended color. Combine colors that are similar in warmth or coolness (such as red and orange, or blue and green). If you layer colors that are opposites (or complementary colors) such as red over green, or blue over orange, the colors may get muddy.

■ *Layering to alter or deepen a hue:* You can change the hue or depth of a color by layering an area of applied color with white before adding another layer of the same color. Apply the two color layers with medium pressure, and the white with hard pressure.

■ *Reserving the highlights:* To create a light area of color within a design, such as a highlight, first apply a layer of white or a pale color to the wood with medium to hard pressure *(photo 8)*. Use a color over the image, to cover the white area with light strokes

8

(photo 9). Use hard pressure to apply a second layer of white over the highlighted area. To create a pure white highlight, leave the white area uncolored.

■ *Creating an antique look:* To create an antique appearance, overlay the edges of the shadows of your design with touches of burnt umber oil pencil.

■ *Creating shadows*: To create shadows you can combine stippling with areas of oil pencil. Make small dots with the woodburner point in the areas that you want to read as shadows before adding pale to dark color *(photo 10).*

Finishing the Oil Pencil Design

After layering colors, use the tip of a cotton swab, an artist's pastel blending stick, or your finger, to blend the

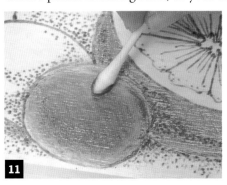

colors and manipulate layers of pigmented wax on the surface *(photo 11).* If you end up with areas of color that you don't want, you'll be able to erase them with the ink end of your eraser, as long as they aren't too dark. If the color is heavily applied, you can often lightly sand it to remove it.

If areas of oil pencil work are left unsealed for long periods of time, the wax tends to float to the surface, leaving a white film called "wax bloom" on the surface. To remove it, wipe the piece with a clean, soft rag. To prevent this, you should spray your oil pencil design with an acrylic sealer to prevent smearing when you've finished it. If you aren't finished with your colored design, but need to leave it for a period of time, seal it with a workable fixative leaving a toothy finish that can be colored over.

TRANSPARENT BLENDING GELS

Transparent blending gels, composed of pigment suspended in clear acrylic gel medium, were originally developed for use on ceramic greenware. They also work well for painting rich areas of color onto wood. They're easy to use because they don't dry quickly, but sit on the surface longer than paints, allowing them to be blended, blotted, or wiped to create different effects.

Blending gels do not run or bleed, and after blotting, you can use water to wipe some of the excess color off of areas that are too heavy. After they dry, erase small mistakes that you don't want with a rubber eraser. Because they are acrylic-based, brushes and containers clean up easily with water.

Use the guidelines below for applying blending gels after you've burned your design and erased any tracing or pencil lines:

■ Use a small brush to paint all areas of the design that are the same color *(photo 12).* Then use a clean, absorbent cloth to gently blot away the excess paint *(photo 13).* (Old, thin washcloths or dishtowels work well for blotting. Keep turning the rag to a clean section as you go along to avoid smearing the surface.) After finishing those areas, move to the next color.

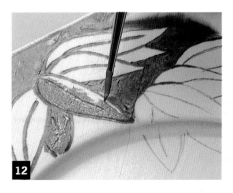

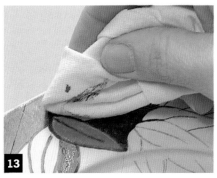

■ If you want to switch colors while painting, simply use another clean brush, or rinse and dry the one you're using.

■ To create a transparent effect, rub off some of the gel after blotting, so that the wood shows through.

■ If you accidentally paint outside the lines of a design, you can remove areas of unwanted paint with a damp cotton swab or cloth before they dry.

After the painting is dry, touch up woodburned lines that have been covered with paint by reburning the design over the paint (*photo 14*).

WOOD STAINS

Some of the projects you'll explore in this book are colored with wood stains after the woodburning is done. Staining can be accomplished by one of two methods:

1. If you find the right color, pre-mixed water-based gel stains are available at art, craft, and hobby stores. Just paint the gel on the wood (*photo 15*), then wipe it down with a clean cloth to reveal the wood grain underneath (*photo 16*). Controlling the placement of gel stains is easy, because they don't run like liquid stains. You'll be able to place different colors of stain on various areas of the design without blurring. Stain one color at a time, and wipe it down before applying the next one.

2. If the desired colors aren't available, mix your own using half acrylic paint and half clear glaze base to create any color that you need. Check the color by trying the mixture on a scrap of wood before using it on your project. Apply the mixture in the same fashion as a gel stain.

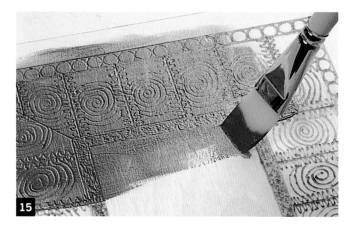

TIP

Be aware that you can damage a section of woodburning if you rub a stain or transparent gel over it without first wiping the surface of the wood. Tiny flakes of ash that rest on the surface after woodburning a design should be wiped off before applying stains or gels. If the woodburned areas lighten after wiping, simply retrace your design with the burner to darken it. Blow away the excess ash of burning until the design is as dark as you want it before you rub a stain or gel on top of it.

Antique woodburned and painted vase with poinsettia design. Purchased in Perth, Australia. Collection of Betty Auth

Diane Peterson (Asheville, North Carolina), Gourds woodburned with controlled-temperature burner. Brown leather dye used on background. Pine needle borders whipstiched on necks

top: **Betty Auth** (Houston, Texas),
Woodburned antique shoe lasts
with added colored pencil
Vivian Williams (Asheville, North Carolina),
Woodburned duck design on plaque
framed with rhododendron branches

center: Antique woodburned pipe rack.
Collection of Betty Auth

bottom: Victorian woodburned boxes.
Collection of Betty Auth

top: **David A. Gregory** (Eldrid, New York), *Harbor Scene*, Woodburned pine enhanced with colored oil pencils and stains

bottom: **Dennis and Vivian Williams** (Asheville, North Carolina), *Rustic Chair*, Chair constructed of rhododendron branches with a woodburned hemlock seat

top: **Bunny DeLorie**,
(Goleta, California)
Fish Tray, Woodburned with
tung oil stains added

bottom: Albanian
woodburned plates, and
painted Dutch wooden
shoe bank with
woodburned accents.
Collection of Betty Auth

top: Woodburned letter holder, and set of woodburned goblets. Collection of Betty Auth

center: Vivian Williams (Asheville, North Carolina), Woodburned design on plaque framed with rhododendron branches

bottom: Betty Auth (Houston, Texas), Woodburned triangular box inspired by an old stencil, and pre-stamped woodburned antique tray.

Butterfly Treasures Box

A hike in the woods or a walk on the beach can fill your pockets with a handful of collected treasures that you can't bear to throw out. This beautiful box makes a great place to store and savor them later.

The butterfly's wings lend themselves to repetitious patterning made with stippling techniques. This project will teach you how to use stippling, repeating lines, and shading effectively.

YOU WILL NEED

Large wooden box, about 9 x 12 x 4 inches (22.5 x 30 x 10 cm)

Fine-grain sandpaper

Masking tape

Design template (page 72)

Graphite paper

Sharp pencil (no. 2)

Eraser

Soft, lintfree cloth

Satin or matte acrylic varnish

Fruitwood or maple gel wood stain

Scissors

Woodburner with large, rounded point and shading point

Cork-backed ruler or other straightedge

¾-inch (1.9 cm) flat, white nylon paintbrush

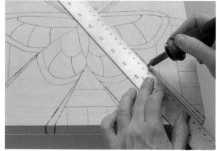

1 Sand the box with fine sandpaper, and round off any sharp edges. Enlarge the template on page 72 to the size indicated. Cut out the design, and tape it to the box's top. Slip graphite paper underneath, and trace the lines with a sharp pencil. Extend the straight, diagonal lines down the side of the lid, as shown. Use a ruler to mark off 1-inch-wide bands in the top section, the right and left center sections, and the bottom section of the design

bordering the butterfly. Make perpendicular marks 1 inch apart inside of each band, as shown. Use the ruler to guide your hand as you burn the straight lines.

2 Insert the large, rounded point, and heat the wood-burner. Outline the butterfly. Use a metal ruler as a guide to burn the radiating lines, including those that extend down onto the sides of the lid. (Allow for the width of the point by placing the ruler next to, not on, the line.) Pull the point toward you as you move it along the edge of the ruler. Burn parallel lines, or a basket weave pattern, in alternating directions within the boxes that form the outer border. Inside the next band, stipple an overall pattern. Inside the band closest to the butterfly, fill in a design by scribbling, or continuously rotating the burning point in small circles.

3 Use the shading point to burn the four triangular bands which radiate out from the butterfly. Leave the rays between these areas and the basket weave unburned. Continue to use the shading point to darken the thorax, or center of the butterfly's body.

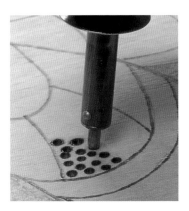

4 To decorate the butterfly's wings, use five different graphic designs. Refer to the photo of the finished design to add large dots, small circles, zigzag lines, spirals, and curving contour lines. Vary

these designs as you choose. Use the eraser to remove all pencil and graphite marks.

5 Use tape to mask the outside edges of the basket weave sections, and paint on a generous coat of maple or fruitwood gel stain. With a clean cloth, wipe off the excess stain so that the burning will show through. Avoid scrubbing so that you won't remove the ash that creates the darkness of the burning. If the stain is too dark, dampen the rag with water, and remove more color. After the stain has dried, remove the tape, mask off the sides of the lid, and stain the bottom half of the box.

6 Remove the masking tape, and paint the inside and outside of the box with two coats of acrylic varnish. Sand lightly between coats.

TIP To lend an element of surprise, treat the inside of the box by painting it a brilliant color before varnishing it. You can also line it with gift wrap, felt, or other fabric.

Holiday Ornaments

Simple geometric motifs burned on wooden shapes make great Christmas tree ornaments. Use our patterns, or make up your own to use on these inexpensive wood pieces—a convenient way to learn techniques before attempting them on a larger piece.

YOU WILL NEED

Wooden shapes, each at least 2 inches (5 cm) in diameter

Very fine sandpaper

Masking tape

Design templates (page 77)

Graphite paper

Sharp pencil (no. 2)

Metal ruler (optional)

Eraser

Gloss acrylic varnish

Large and medium jump rings

Decorative chain

Ornament hangers

Scissors

Woodburner with large and small rounded points

½ or ¾-inch (1.3 or 1.9 cm) flat, white nylon paintbrush

Needle-nose pliers

Wire cutters

TIP Look for wooden shapes with holes aready drilled near the edge for attaching hangers. If unavailable, buy or cut round shapes, then drill holes near the edge with a ¼-inch (.6 cm) drill bit.

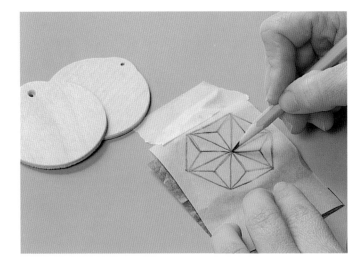

3 Use the woodburner to cover the edges with parallel lines to create a coin-edged effect. Use the gray end of the eraser to remove all pencil and graphite marks. Finish cleaning the surface with the white end of the eraser. Wipe away all dust.

1 Sand the wooden shapes with very fine sandpaper in the direction of the grain. Round off the edges as desired. Brush away any dust. Enlarge the templates on page 77 to the size indicated. Cut out each design. Center and tape a design on a wooden shape. Slip graphite paper underneath, and trace the lines with a sharp pencil. Remove the designs, and darken any lines that are unclear with a pencil.

4 Use wire cutters to cut a length of chain for hanging the ornament. Pry open a jump ring with two pairs of needle-nose pliers. Attach the chain to the ring.

2 Insert the large, rounded point, and heat the woodburner. Outline the designs, and fill in the backgrounds with shading or other woodburning techniques, such as stippling, scribbles, or parallel lines. If the wood you're using is very soft, or you want to burn more intricate patterns, switch to the small, rounded point.

5 Place another jump ring in the hole in the ornament, and attach the chain to it by its jump ring. (Using two jump rings together allows the ornament to swing freely.) Use wire cutters to cut the chain to the length that you desire. Place another jump ring on the opposite end of the chain for attaching an ornament hanger. Paint the ornaments with two coats of glossy acrylic varnish. Use masking tape to attach the chains to the edge of a shelf so that the ornaments can hang freely while the varnish dries.

Heartfelt Bird Home

Any bird would appreciate having this pretty roof over its head! This is a great beginner's project, and burning the dots around the hearts is like magic when you see little puffs of smoke rising up from the wood!

1 Sand the birdhouse and roof with medium sandpaper in the direction of the grain. Round off any sharp edges, and sand inside the holes in the front. Brush away the dust.

2 Enlarge the template on page 73 to the size indicated. Cut out each of the motifs. Tape the shingled motif to one side of the slanted roof. Slip graphite paper underneath it, and trace the design with a pencil. After removing the design, darken any unclear lines with a pencil. Use the same template to transfer a shingle design to the other side of the roof. Transfer the rest of the designs to the front and sides of the birdhouse using the same process.

3 Insert the large, rounded point, and heat the woodburner. Outline the designs on the front, sides, and roof. (Since pine is often a rough and irregular wood, you may need to burn the lines two or three times to darken them. If they are a bit sketchy looking, don't worry.)

4 Add round dots around the drawn hearts on each side and around the heart-shaped holes on the front. To do this, hold the burner upright, and touch the wood with the full circle of the point until a bit of smoke rises.

5 Continue burning lines, including the textural ones drawn within the grass and branches. When burning is complete, use the gray end of the eraser to remove all pencil and graphite marks. Finish cleaning the surface with the white end of the eraser. Wipe away any eraser crumbs.

6 Use the ¾-inch (1.9 cm) flat brush to apply matte varnish to all surfaces, including the edges of the openings in the front and the removable panel on the bottom of the birdhouse.

TIP If you would like to use the birdhouse outside, apply two or three coats of exterior acrylic varnish to the inside and outside. Sand lightly between coats.

Fish Bowl

*This powerful yet simple design conforms to the curves of a shallow
wooden bowl. You'll learn the tricks of transferring a design to a
curved surface by using non-fusible interfacing and a ballpoint pen.*

YOU WILL NEED

Maple or oak bowl, about 8 inches (20 cm) in diameter

Transparent ruler

Design template (page 74)

Non-fusible interfacing

Ballpoint pen

Masking tape

Graphite paper

Sharp pencil (no. 2)

Eraser

Matte or satin acrylic varnish

Scissors

Woodburner with large, rounded point

¾-inch (1.9 cm) flat,
white nylon paintbrush

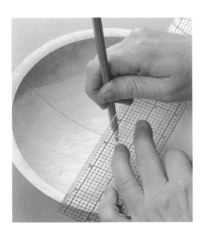

1 Use a ruler to draw two lines that cross the center of the bowl and divide it into four equal segments. These lines will be used as guides for placing the patterns on the rounded surface of the bowl.

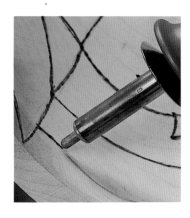

4 Use the finished piece pictured on page 30 as a guide to draw curving lines with a pencil around the fish. Insert the large, rounded point, and heat the wood-burner. Burn the outlines of the design.

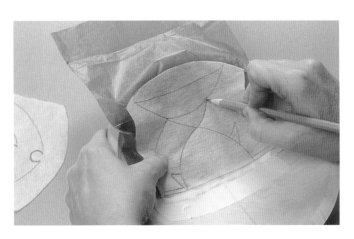

5 Fill in the fish body and the outermost border around the bowl with scribbling. Stipple the blank

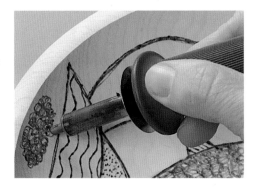

portion of the fish tail with small dots. Erase all the pencil and graphite marks.

2 Enlarge the template on page 74 to the size indicated. Trace it onto non-fusible interfacing, using the ballpoint pen to avoid tearing. Cut out the fish design, leaving at least a ½-inch border around it. Then cut the design in half along the centerline of the fish. Align one half of the design with the bowl's centerline, and tape it in place. Slip graphite paper underneath it, and transfer the lines with the ballpoint pen. After removing the design, darken any unclear lines with a pencil.

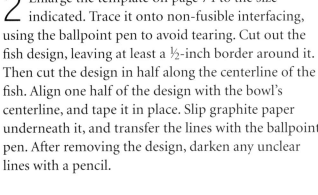

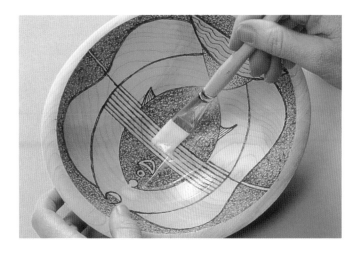

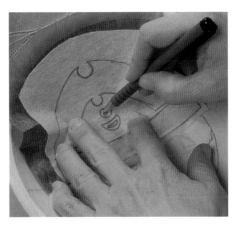

3 Turn the bowl, and repeat this process to add the other half of the design.

6 Varnish the entire bowl, inside and out, with a coat of acrylic varnish. Sand the bowl lightly, and then apply another coat.

VARIATION Use the same method described above to transfer the snake design on page 74. Center the snake, then repeat the accompanying motif four times around the edges. Connect the repeated motifs with freehand curved lines.

African Safari Planter Box

Striped zebras and funky elephants cavort around the sides of this functional planter. The box is made of rough pine, which lends itself to large, primitive, stylized designs. By moving a large, rounded point slowly over the wood's toothy surface, you'll be able to fill in the outlines of the designs, and bring the animals to life!

YOU WILL NEED

Wooden planter box, about 9 inches (22.5 cm) square

Medium-grain sandpaper or sanding block

Masking tape

Design templates (page 78)

Graphite paper

Sharp pencil (no. 2)

Eraser

Exterior acrylic varnish, satin or matte

Scissors

Woodburner with large, rounded point

¾-inch (⅑ cm) flat, white nylon paintbrush

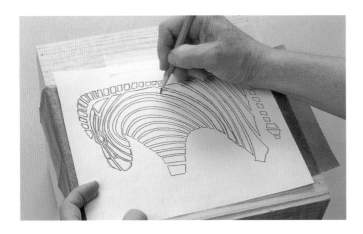

1 Leave the surface of this piece unsanded except for the sharp edges, which you can round off with a sanding block or medium sandpaper. Enlarge the templates on page 78 to the size indicated. Cut them out. Tape the zebra in place on the side of the box, slip graphite paper underneath, and trace it with a sharp pencil. After removing the design, darken any unclear lines with a pencil.

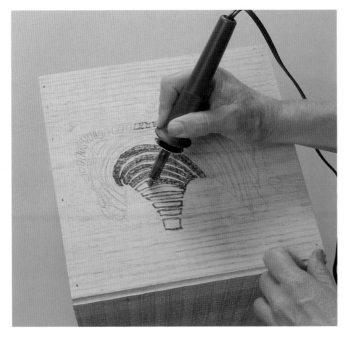

2 Insert the large, rounded point, and heat the woodburner. Outline the design. Fill in the dark areas of the design by moving the woodburner back and forth and in small circles. To darken hard-to-burn areas, hold the burner upright and burn large dots.

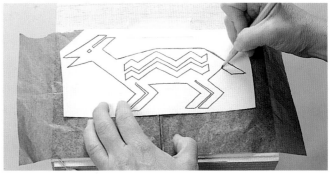

3 Trace another animal onto a side of the planter.

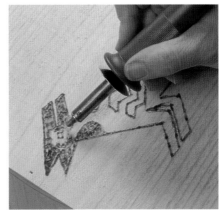

4 Burn it using the large, rounded point.

5 Trace and burn the other two animals on the remaining sides of the planter, and burn them in the same fashion. After all the designs are burned, brush on at least two coats of exterior varnish, matte or satin.

TIP Line the bottom of the planter with foil or a square cake pan before placing a plant in it. To preserve the wood, take the plant out before watering it.

Piney Woods Table

The simple oval shapes of pine cones on branches are echoed by the top of this side table, which fits into almost any décor. This is a gratifying project for beginners—it looks more complicated than it is!

NOTE Before assembling the table according to the directions enclosed with it, transfer and burn the designs onto the top, legs, and brace. After completion of the design, you can varnish the pieces and the wooden screws individually, or varnish the whole table after it is assembled.

1 Sand the table in the direction of the grain, rounding off the sharp edges. Brush away all dust. Enlarge the template on page 76 to the size indicated. Cut out the motifs for the table's top, legs, and brace. Tape the branch design in place on the tabletop, and slip graphite paper underneath. Trace the lines with a sharp pencil. Use a straightedge or ruler to trace the pine needles. Remove the design and graphite paper. Use a pencil to darken any lines that are unclear.

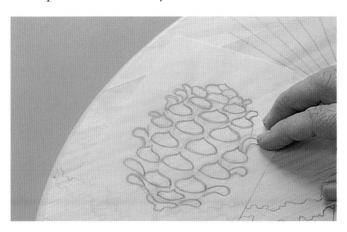

2 Position a pine cone design on the blank stem of a branch, and tape it in place, so that the lines you've already drawn meet the base of the cone.

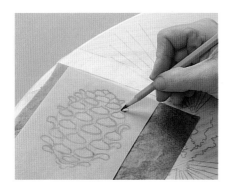

3 Insert graphite paper underneath, and trace the cone. Repeat this process, adding small and large cones to the branches.

4 Insert the large, rounded point, and heat the woodburner. Outline the designs. Use a metal ruler to burn the straight lines that indicate pine needles. Darken the branches and the oval background of each pine cone, using a continuous back and forth or circular motion with the burner's point. (This movement is similar to scribbling with a pencil.) When finished, use the gray end of the eraser to remove all pencil and graphite marks. Finish cleaning the surface with the white end of the eraser. Wipe off the eraser crumbs.

5 Transfer the branch design for the table leg, and add pine cones after you've established its placement, using the same method described for the table's top. Flip the tracing paper over, and trace a mirror image of the design on the other table leg. Burn the designs as described for the table's top. Transfer and burn the final design on the bracing shelf. Paint the table, either in sections or assembled, with a coat of satin acrylic varnish. Sand it lightly after it dries, and apply a second coat of varnish.

TIP To give this table a rich, warm look, stain it with maple or fruitwood gel wood stain before varnishing.

Nana's Cherry Box

This box is a replica of one that has been in my family for over 90 years. My grandmother burned the original prestamped design while attending business school in San Francisco in 1906. Since it happened to be the year of the San Francisco fire, we thought that Nana was clever to blame the fire on the earthquake instead of her woodburner!

YOU WILL NEED

Hinged basswood box, 8 x 3 x 5 inches (20 x 7.5 x 12.5 cm)	Matte acrylic varnish
Fine-grain sandpaper	16mm unfinished wooden bead
Design templates (page 70)	Scissors
Masking tape	Woodburner with large, rounded point and small, rounded point
Tracing paper or other thin paper	
Graphite paper	¾-inch (1.9 cm) flat, white nylon paintbrush
Sharp pencil (No. 2)	¾-inch (1.9 cm) brass wood screw with shaft to fit through bead hole
Eraser	
Soft, lintfree cloth	Screwdriver

1 Sand the box in the direction of the grain, rounding off any sharp edges. Brush away the dust. Enlarge the templates on page 70 to the size indicated. Cut them out. Tape the box shut on the sides with small

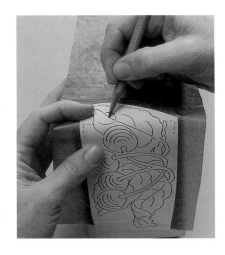

pieces of masking tape. Tape the top design in place first, and slip graphite paper underneath. Trace the lines with a pencil. Remove the design and graphite paper. Darken the lines with a pencil if needed. Repeat this process for the design on the front of the box. Trace the design for the end of the box, and allow the tip of the leaf to wrap around the front. Flip the tracing paper over, and transfer the reversed design to the other end of the box.

original lines on the cherries. Burn short parallel lines to cover the background around and between the designs. To do this, keep the woodburner point moving back and forth in short strokes, without lifting the tip from the surface.

4 Using the small, rounded point, burn short, parallel, coin-edge lines along the rounded edges of the box. Darken the small triangles which are formed at each corner where the edges meet.

After finishing the design, use the gray end of the eraser to remove all pencil and graphite marks. Finish cleaning the surface with the white end of the eraser. Wipe off the eraser crumbs.

2 Insert the large, rounded point and heat the woodburner. Outline all of the designs, including the main shading lines on the cherries and the main lines of the leaves.

5 Paint the inside and outside of the box with a coat of matte acrylic varnish. After the varnish dries, lightly sand the box before applying the other coat of varnish. Stain or paint the wooden bead, then screw it into the lid for a handle.

TIP To treat the inside box edges as a part of the design, continue the design inside the edges. To keep the inside edges of the box clean while burning the outside, lay strips of masking tape where you don't want to burn a design.

3 Switch to the small, rounded point. Burn the more detailed shadow and texture lines on the leaves, and more texture lines between the

Memory Album

Keep your photos safe and sound, like your grandmother did, with this updated version of a "memory album." Burn the cover with a simple border to frame a family photo, then stain it with earth-toned wood stains, and you'll have a keepsake to pass down to your children.

YOU WILL NEED

Wooden memory album cover to fit 8½ x 11-inch (21.3 x 27.5 cm) pages

Fine-grain sandpaper

Design template (page 77)

Masking tape

Graphite paper

Sharp pencil (no. 2)

Photograph of your choice, vertical format, photocopied and sized to 3½ x 5 inches (8.8 x 12.5 cm)

Eraser

Soft, lintfree cloth

Walnut and cherry gel wood stains

Matte acrylic varnish

Scissors

Screwdriver

Woodburner with large, rounded point

Craft knife with sharp blade

¾-inch (1.9 cm) flat white nylon paintbrush

TIP Use a photocopy for your album cover image rather than the original. Not only will you save the original, but a photocopy will work better than an original photograph. Copy the photo onto satin finish inkjet or laser copier paper using a photocopier or a computer scanner. Size it to a vertical 3½ x 5-inch (8.8 x 12.5 cm) format. (Your photo copy center can do this for you.)

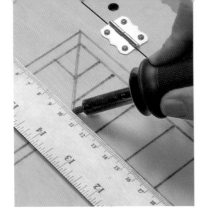

1 Remove the two screws that hold the cover together, but leave the hinges in place. Sand the wood with fine sandpaper in the direction of the grain. Enlarge the template on page 77 to the size indicated. Cut out the design, and tape it on the center of the front cover. Slip graphite paper underneath before tracing the design with a sharp pencil. Darken any unclear lines with the pencil once you remove the design. Insert the large, rounded point, and heat the woodburner. Use a ruler as a guide to trace the straight lines of the design.

2 Use the same point to add zigzag lines across the straight dividing lines. Add small circles within the band around the frame, and spirals inside the rectangular portions. Solidly fill the inside border with dark burning by rotating the point in small continuous circles. Use the eraser to remove all pencil and graphite marks.

3 Cover the outer, unburned border of the album cover with masking tape to shield it while staining the frame. Use cherry wood gel stain to cover the entire center portion of the album cover, including the part you've burned and the photo opening. Immediately

after applying the gel, use a clean cloth to lightly wipe off excess color and allow the woodburning to show through. If you dim any of the woodburned lines while rubbing the surface, you can retouch the lines after the stain has dried. If the color is too dark, dip the cloth in water and remove more of the stain.

4 After the center area dries, remove the masking tape around the edge. Place masking tape on the stained portion along the line that separates it from the outer unstained areas. Paint walnut gel stain on the outer edges of the album, the inside, and the back cover. Wipe the excess stain away. (Allow each side to dry before painting another one.) After the stain dries, remove the masking tape.

5 Trim the photo to fit the center opening in the frame. Paint a smooth, ample coat of acrylic varnish in the center opening on the cover, and let it dry a few seconds. Paint another coat over the first one. Turn the photo over and paint the back with a full, even coat of varnish.

6 Lay the photo in place, aligning the edges. Smooth it to remove any air bubbles. Paint a coat of varnish over the front of the photo, using the varnish to further adhere the photo to the album. Smooth away air bubbles, allow it to dry. Paint the inside and outside of the album with two coats of matte acrylic varnish. Sand lightly between coats.

Patterned Frame

You can adorn any unfinished flat frame with abstract ornamentation. This design is based on a simple grid that you'll burn and then fill with repeating spiral shapes. The overall patterning lends the frame a rich, ethnic look.

YOU WILL NEED

Flat wooden frame with an outside measurement of 8½ x 11 inches (21.3 X 27.5 cm) and a 5½ x 8¼-inch (13.8 x 20.6 cm) opening

Fine-grain sandpaper

Design template (page 77)

Masking tape

Graphite paper

Sharp pencil (no. 2)

Eraser

Soft, lintfree cloth

Maple gel wood stain

Satin or matte acrylic varnish

Woodburner with small, rounded point

Scissors

¾-inch (1.9 cm) flat, white nylon paintbrush

1 Sand the frame first, rounding off any sharp edges. Enlarge the template on page 77 to the size indicated. Cut it out, and leave a border around the design. Tape it to the top of the frame, and slip graphite paper underneath it. Trace the lines with a sharp pencil to transfer them. Next, use a pencil to draw the scalloped lines around the border. Don't worry about making each one exactly the same. This finished pattern has a look of one that is hand drawn.

2 Insert the small, rounded point, and heat the woodburner. Burn the lines of the design that you've drawn so far.

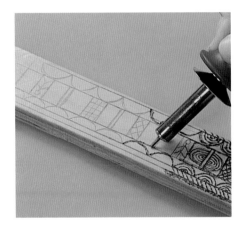

3 Using the photo of the finished piece on page 40 as a guide, burn freehand repeating curved lines inside the scalloped border. Then burn the repeating spiral shapes in the inner border of the frame. (Try out a

spiral on a piece of scrap wood first if you're uncomfortable with drawing it without practice.)

4 Use a ¾-inch (1.9 cm) flat paintbrush to paint maple gel stain on the frame, one side at a time.

5 With the cloth, wipe off the excess stain so the woodburning shows through. If it is too dark, wet the rag slightly, and rub some of it off. Repeat this process for all sides. Stain the outside edges and the inner edges. After the stain is dry, paint the entire frame with two coats of varnish.

Ladder-back Chair

Watch the mountains change as you move up the rungs of this ladder-back chair. The motifs evolve from a simple outline to shaded, dimensional forms, symbolizing transitions from the bareness of winter to the fullness of summer. The techniques used to add shading to the mountains range from simple stippling to hatching.

YOU WILL NEED

Oak or birch, unfinished ladderback chair

Fine-grain sandpaper

Design template (page 75)

Masking tape

Graphite paper

Sharp pencil (no. 2)

Eraser

Maple or cherry gel wood stain

Clear gel faux glaze base

Satin or matte acrylic varnish

Scissors

Woodburner with large, rounded point

¾-inch (1.9 cm) flat, white nylon paintbrush

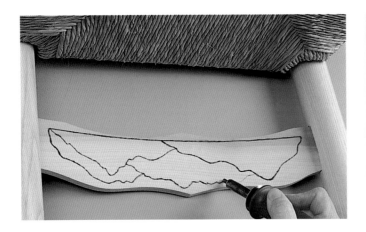

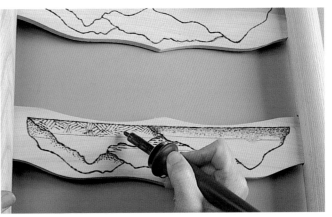

1 Before beginning work on the chair, place it on its back on a table so that it is easier to work on. Enlarge the template on page 75 to the size indicated. Cut it out, and tape it to the bottom rung. Slip graphite paper underneath the design, and trace over the lines with a sharp pencil. Transfer the same design to the other three rungs. Insert the large rounded point, and heat the woodburner. Burn the outlines of the designs on each rung.

3 As you ascend the rungs of the chair, burn the designs higher up each mountain, and slightly darker. Allow the patterns to fade slightly as you move up each mountain.

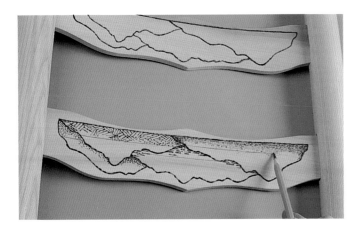

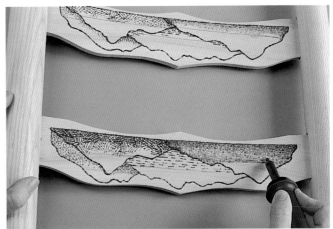

2 On the second rung up from the seat of the chair, sketch in a horizontal pencil line about an inch (2.5 cm) up from the base of each mountain. On the third rung up, pencil a line slightly further up, or about 1½ inches (3.8 cm) from the base of each mountain. Burn a variety of patterns between the base of each mountain and the lines that you've sketched. Use any patterns that you choose (see pages 14 and 15 for descriptions) including hatching, parallel lines, stippling, and dashed lines.

4 On the final rung, fill the mountains with patterning. After you've finished burning the design, stain the chair with a mixture of a small amount of cherry or maple gel wood stain in clear glaze. (Test your mixture on a blank piece of wood, or on part of the wood that won't show later, to see if you like the color and darkness of it.) After the mixture dries, coat the chair and rungs with a coat of varnish. Sand lightly before applying another coat of varnish.

Folding Screen

Light up a corner, or hide your most disorganized piles, with this three-part screen.
The symmetrical, repeated design that is burned at the top of each section coordinates
with the fabric that makes up the curtains. Use our design, or pick out a fabric with a
motif, and use it as inspiration for your own woodburned decoration.

1 Enlarge the template on page 71 to the size indicated. Cut out the scalloped design, and tape it in the center of the upper portion of one of the three sections of the screen. Slip graphite

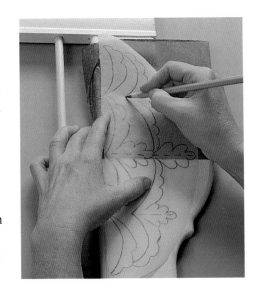

paper underneath the design. Trace the lines of the design with a sharp pencil. Use the same design to repeat this process for the other two sections.

2 Insert the large, rounded point, and heat the woodburner. Burn the outlines of the designs on all three sections.

3 Stipple small dots under the curving lines at the base of each design, and allow them to fade out at the bottom.

4 Fill in the tree-shaped designs with dashed diagonal lines, keeping them uniform as you add them to each of the three sections. (Sketch in pencil guidelines if you need them.) Continue to use the large, rounded point, and fill in the center of each design with scribbled marks made by moving the burner's point in continuous, small circles. Darken the center sections as uniformly as possible.

5 Paint the sections that you've burned with leaf green transparent blending gel. Use a soft cloth to rub away the excess gel, and leave a green stain on the wood. Rub gold highlights on the tops of the designs with the end of a cotton swab. Stain the screen with a mixture of a small amount of brown gel

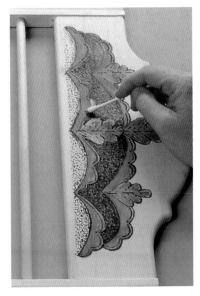

wood stain in clear glaze. After the mixture dries, coat the screen with a coat of varnish. Sand lightly before applying another coat. After everything dries, stretch fabric curtains on the dowels.

Playful Pins

These three pins begin with a wooden form onto which a design is burned. Use the supplies listed below to complete the body of each pin. (Separate supplies are also listed for each style of beading.) The beading techniques are interchangeable, and you can transfer them from one form to another, or mix them on the same piece.

Before beginning these projects, use an electric or cordless drill with a ⅛-inch (.3 cm) drill bit to drill holes along the edges for attaching the beads. Refer to the photos of the finished pieces for placement of the holes. Drill the holes about ⅛-inch (.3 cm) from the edges. This distance will allow you enough room to attach the jump rings without splitting the wood.

YOU WILL NEED FOR EACH PROJECT

Wooden heart, hand, or asymmetrical star

Electric or cordless drill with ⅛-inch (.3 cm) drill bit

Fine-grain sandpaper

Design templates (page 72)

Graphite paper

Sharp pencil (no. 2)

Eraser

Soft, lintfree cloth

Walnut and maple gel wood stain

Satin acrylic varnish

White craft glue or hot glue gun

1½- or 2-inch (3.8 or 5 cm) pinback

Scissors

Woodburner with small, rounded point

¾- and ¼-inch (1.9 and .6 cm) flat, white nylon paintbrushes

Two pairs of needle-nose pliers

One pair of round-nose pliers

YOU WILL NEED FOR THE HEART PIN

About 24-inch (60 cm) length of 20-24 gauge brass wire (fine enough to pass through holes)

Variety of red glass beads, both clear and opaque

Heart Pin

This pin has beads "sewn" around the edges of it with wire. Although the final product looks complex, it's easy to do.

1 Enlarge the heart template on page 72 to the size indicated. Cut the design out, align it with the edges of the wooden heart, and slide a small piece of graphite paper between the heart and the design. Use a sharp pencil to trace the lines of the design onto the heart. Remove the design, and darken any lines that are unclear. Burn the design with the small rounded point. Erase all pencil and graphite marks.

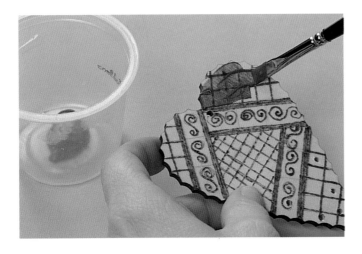

2 Apply maple stain with the small paintbrush to all areas except the crisscrossing bands.

3 Use a clean cloth to blot the stain. Repeat this process to apply walnut gel stain to the bands. Continue to use the cloth to rub away enough stain that the woodburned patterns show through. Apply stain to the back of the heart, blot it, and rub it. After the stain dries, apply two coats of varnish to the back and front of the heart.

4 Use the round-nose pliers to bend several small circles into the end of the brass wire.

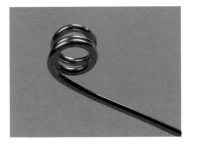

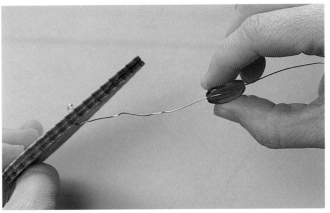

5 Locate the third hole up from the bottom on either side of the heart. Push the straight end of the wire from the back of the heart and through this hole. Pull it out the other side until the loop that you created stops it. Thread a bead onto the wire, and push it down to the face of the heart.

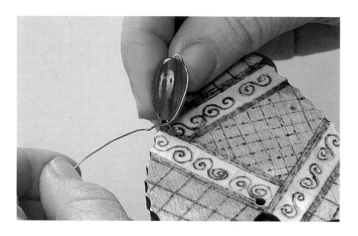

6 Wrap and crisscross the wire around the bead two or three times to secure it. The bead should rest near the edge of the heart, without the wire being so tight that it might snap later.

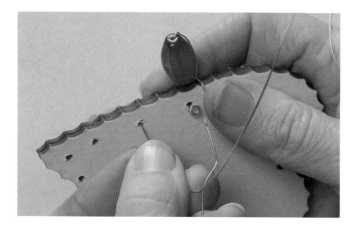

7 Pull the wire to the back of the heart, and push it up through the next hole. Following the same

process described in step six, add six more beads on a continuous piece of wire until you've arrived at the hole that is across from the first one you strung. After stringing the bead for this last hole, wind the wire around the bead. Tie off the wire on the front of the heart by making small circles in it with the round-nose pliers before clipping it with wire cutters. To add the bead at the top of the heart, cut a 6-inch length of wire and bend several circles in the end. String on a bead or two, push the wire through the front of the top hole, and loosely wrap and twist the wire around the bead. Add another bead, and tie off the wire with a couple of small circles. Now that the beads are in place, twist and turn them until you like the way they look. Glue a pinback in a horizontal position above center on the back of the heart. After the glue dries, try the pin on and make certain that no beads and wire are positioned in such a way that they snag your clothing. If they do, bend them into a different position, away from your clothing.

Star Pin

When you make this pin, you'll use eye pins to attach the beads. The dangling effect that they create is a perfect complement for the points of the stars. (Cats and babies will be fascinated by the moving beads when you wear this pin! So keep a safe distance!)

YOU WILL NEED

Five 2-inch (5 cm) long eye pins

5 small brass jump rings

5 small crystal leaf beads

1 1/2-2-inch (3.8 to 5 cm) long pinback

White glue or hot glue gun

1 Enlarge the template on page 72 to the size indicated. Trace onto the form with a sharp pencil.

2 Burn the design with the small, rounded point of the woodburner.

3 Refer to the photo of the final piece, and stain the points of the star and other darkened areas with maple gel stain. Blot and rub the excess stain away with a clean cloth. Stain the back of the pin. Stain the contrasting areas with walnut gel stain. After the stain dries, paint the pin with two coats of varnish. Attach a crystal dangle leaf to the circular end of the eye pin with a jump ring. String a yellow bead, a crystal bead, and another yellow bead onto the eye pin, then push the straight end of it through one of the holes on the front of the star. On the back of the star, use round-nose pliers to bend small circles in the straight end of the eye pin. This loop on the back will allow the beads to dangle without coming out of the hole. Repeat this process on the other four points of the star. Glue a pinback in a horizontal position above center on the back of the star.

Heart in Hand Pin

This pin uses jump rings to attach the pearl drop beads that hang from the fingertips and edge of the hand. The pearls provide an elegant, dressy touch to the pin.

YOU WILL NEED

10 large brass jump rings

10 pearl-drop beads with hanging loops inserted in tops

Small pinback to fit across the wrist of the hand

1 Enlarge the template on page 72 to the size indicated. Trace onto the form with a sharp pencil.

2 Burn the design with the small, rounded point.

3 Apply maple stain with the paintbrush to the fingertips and edge of the hand, leaving the other areas unstained. Use a clean cloth to blot the stain. Continue to use the cloth to rub away enough stain that the woodburned patterns show through. (Take care not to blur the stain into the unpainted areas.) Apply stain to the back of the heart, blot it, and rub it. After the stain dries, apply two coats of varnish to the back and front of the hand. Open a large jump ring by holding the ring with one pair of pliers and opening it sideways with the other. Push it through a hole, and close it with the pliers. Attach rings in this fashion to the rest of the holes on the hand. Open a second jump ring, and loop it through one of the attached jump rings. Before closing it, add a dangle pearl to it. Use pliers to close the ring. Continue this process to attach pearls to the other fingers. Glue the pinback to the top of the back in a horizontal position, allowing the fingers to point downward.

Drapery Rod and Finials

Spruce up draperies with a set of finials and tiebacks burned with simple geometric designs, flowers, or a motif from your curtain fabric. These unusual additions to your windows will add a distinctive touch to any room of your house.

3 Pencil a wavy line around the base of the finial to mark where the design will end. Switch to the shading point, and burn the background behind the flowers to this line.

1 Enlarge the flower templates on page 70 to the size indicated. Use a ballpoint pen to trace the individual flower designs onto non-fusible interfacing so the patterns will be flexible while you're transferring them to the rounded surface of each finial. Tape one of the flower designs to the finial, and use the pen and a piece of graphite paper to transfer it. Repeat this process, spacing the flowers randomly on the surface.

4 With a pencil, sketch four crossing lines that span the center section of the drapery tieback. (Draw these lines to mimic the sections of an eight-piece pie.) Draw leaf-shaped petals on the outside portion of the finial that intersect these lines. Mark 16 dots around the outermost edge of the tieback. Insert the small, rounded point, and burn the lines that you've drawn. Add squiggly lines with the small point in the centers of the petals and the pie-shaped sections. Switch to the large, rounded point, and burn the dots around the perimeter of the tieback.

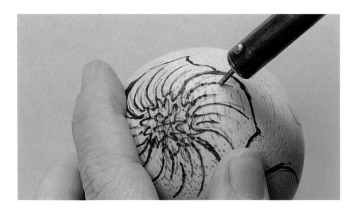

2 Insert the large, rounded point into the wood-burner before heating it. Burn over the outlines of the flowers. Switch to the small rounded point, and add more details, such as additional curved lines on the petals.

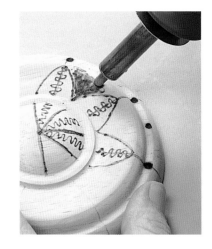

5 Use the large point to add dark, solid shading between the petals. Screw in the small wooden section that comes in the tieback's package, and use it for a handle to hold it while you paint it with two coats of matte or satin varnish.

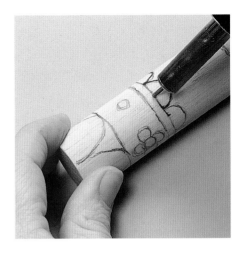

7 Insert the small, rounded point, and burn the linear parts of the design. Switch to the large, rounded point, and fill in the dark background areas. Attach the finials to the ends of the rod, and apply at least two coats of acrylic varnish to the whole assemblage.

6 Cut the rod to the width of your window plus 6 inches (15 cm). Lightly sand the cut edges and down the shaft several inches in the direction of the grain. On a sheet of lined notebook paper, make pencil marks to indicate where you want to place burned lines that circle the shaft. These will be used as guidelines for marking the rod. Lay the rod next to the paper, and slowly turn it, marking it with the pencil as you go around. Add geometric shapes with the pencil between the lines. (You can vary this design in any way that you like.)

TIP Be sure the finials are real wood, not resin or other imitation wood, and that there is no varnish or other finish on them. Old wooden finials can be recycled, but you must remove all residue of old paint or varnish.

Try out other simple designs to decorate finials.

Seaside Bath Accessory

Convert a cute doll desk into a convenient, decorative bath accessory to hold soaps and other toiletries. Burn the outlines of the shells, stipple in small dots for shading, add a subtle background of white behind them, and you'll have a piece that makes your bathroom unique!

Hinged wooden doll desk,
10 x 14 x 7 inches
(25 x 35 x 17.5 cm)

Fine-grain sandpaper

Masking tape

Design templates (page 71)

Graphite paper

Sharp pencil (no. 2)

Eraser

Soft lintfree cloth

Matte acrylic varnish

White acrylic paint

Clear faux finish glaze base

Scissors

Woodburner with large, rounded point
and small, rounded point

½-inch (1.3 cm) flat paintbrush

¾-inch (1.9 cm) flat paintbrush

Small, round, white nylon paintbrush

1 Sand the desk, and round off the sharp edges. Brush away the dust. Enlarge the template on page 71 to the size indicated. Cut out each of the motifs. Tape the large shell motif in the center of the desk's lid, and slip graphite paper underneath. Trace the lines with a sharp pencil. Remove the template and graphite paper, and check the lines for accuracy. Darken them with a pencil if needed. Repeat this process for the two shell motifs on the outside of the lid, and the shell arrangement inside.

3 Use the ½-inch (1.3 cm) flat paintbrush to paint the shells with two coats of matte varnish to protect them from an application of white background paint. Pour several tablespoons of faux glaze base into a container, and add about half as much white acrylic paint. Stir well. Use the ¾-inch (1.9 cm) flat brush to paint the background with the mixture, working on about half the surface at a time. Wipe off excess paint mixture as necessary, and rub down lightly with a clean cloth. When completely dry, paint all surfaces with two coats of the varnish.

4 On the inside of the box, paint the shells with a mixture of half white acrylic and half clear glaze base.

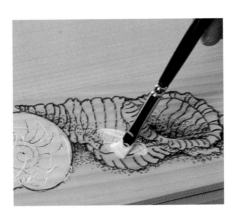

2 Insert the small, rounded point, and heat the woodburner. Outline the designs. Use the same point to scribble the darkest shadows inside the shells. Stipple areas that look like sand and shadows underneath the shells. Switch to the large, rounded point, darken the shadowed area where each shell meets the sand, and reinforce the depth of the shadow inside each shell where it curves inward. Use the gray end of the eraser to remove all pencil and graphite marks. Finish cleaning the surface with the white end of the eraser. Wipe the surface clean.

5 Gently rub off the excess paint with a lintfree cloth. Allow the paint to dry. Varnish over the entire surface, inside and out.

Found Materials

Ever wondered what to do with that nice piece of driftwood that you couldn't resist picking up on the beach last summer but is now taking up space on the floor of a closet? Rough wood found in nature such as driftwood or cypress stumps can be burned to make decorative additions to a shelf or mantel. Old, weather-worn barn slats or pieces of a picket fence can be interesting to burn, too. If you're using wood that might have been treated with preservatives or paint, test-burn a small area of it first to see if you detect noxious fumes. If there are, make certain that you burn the piece outside or in a well-ventilated area.

The three examples that follow will give you ideas to get you started. Since no two pieces of found material are alike, you won't be able to replicate these designs exactly.

YOU WILL NEED

Pieces of found wood such as driftwood or old slats from a barn

Sharp pencil (no. 2)

Woodburner with a large, rounded point, a small, rounded point, and a shading point

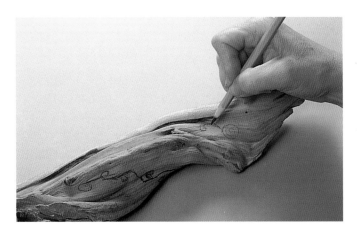

1 Use a pencil to draw small curlicues that follow the curves of the wood on a piece of driftwood.

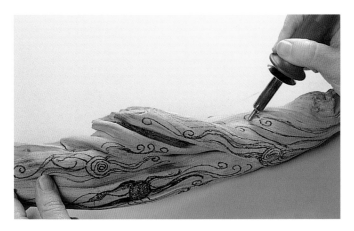

2 Insert the large, rounded point, and heat the woodburner. Burn the curlicue designs that you've sketched on the wood, and add others as you go along until you're satisfied with your design.

3 For another idea, use a discarded portion of the top of a picket fence board as a surface on which

to burn a simple vine pattern. Sketch a curving line on the board for the stem. Burn this line with the large, rounded point.

4 Add leaves on either side of the vine by holding the flat portion of the shading point to the board and rocking it gently without moving it. Wait until you see a small puff of smoke rise, then lift the point straight up. (Practice on a scrap of wood first to get a feel for moving the point back and forth.) If the wood is particularly rough, and doesn't darken adequately on the first burn, repeat this step.

5 On a piece of cypress or other smooth, soft wood, you can create a more complex design. This design was first sketched on the surface, and then burned using small and large rounded points.

Lotus Flower Plate

The ancient lotus plant, a symbol of purity and rebirth in Asian cultures, adorns this elegant, decorative plate. The wide borders provide a perfect background for the simple, curving lines of this design, which show the pink-flowered lotus plant emerging from water. You'll be amazed at how easy and fun it is to add color to this piece with an array of transparent blending gels.

YOU WILL NEED

8-inch (20 cm) basswood octagonal-shaped plate

Fine-grain sandpaper

Design templates (page 70)

Masking tape

Graphite paper

Sharp pencil (No. 2)

Eraser

Soft, lintfree cloth

Bronze acrylic paint

Transparent blending gels: turquoise, rouge, light green, golden yellow, white

Matte acrylic varnish

Scissors

Woodburner with small, rounded point and shading point

¾-inch (1.9 cm) flat, white nylon paintbrush

Small, round paintbrush

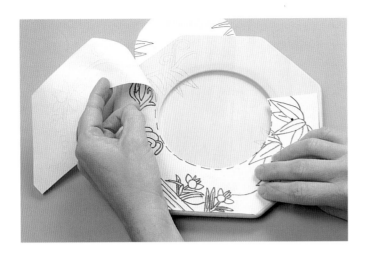

woodburner, and insert the shading point. Lay the shading point flat on the surface of the wood, and make small, continuous circles on the surface to create a deep brown background. After finishing all parts of the design, use the eraser to remove all pencil and graphite marks. Wipe off the eraser crumbs.

1 Sand the plate in the direction of the wood grain. Make sure that you smooth the curved edges. Enlarge the templates on page 70 to the size indicated. Cut the designs out, leaving a border around them. Tape the rim design to the plate with masking tape before slipping the graphite paper underneath. Go over lines of the design with a sharp pencil. Remove the design and graphite paper. Darken the lines with a pencil if needed. Repeat this process for transferring the plate's center design, matching the tips of the leaves to the rest of the design.

4 Using the small, round brush, paint the leaves, flowers, and waves of the design with transparent blending gels, working on a section at a time.

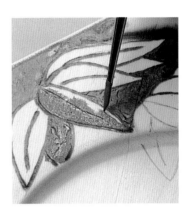

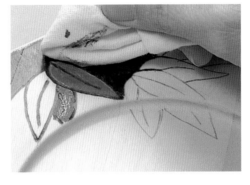

5 After painting an area, blot it with the lintfree cloth to remove excess paint from the surface. Rub away as much color as you would like, allowing the wood grain and burned design to show through.

2 Insert the large, rounded point into the woodburner before heating it. Outline all designs, moving the point at about half the speed of a writing pen.

3 Apply strips of masking tape to the plate's edges to mask them during the process of burning shaded areas on the plate's rim. Use pliers to unscrew the rounded point from the

6 Retouch the woodburning if any lines are obscured by the paint. Using the ¾-inch (1.9 cm) flat brush, paint the plate, back and front, with a coat of matte acrylic varnish. After it dries, sand it lightly before applying a second coat.

Victorian Shoe Last

A hundred years ago, they were used for shaping and repairing shoes... today, you can use an antique shoe last as a whimsical form to decorate. After sanding off the varnish, add designs in any order to this simple shape. Use our selection of templates, and come up with your own creative combination of designs. Then color them with simple-to-use transparent blending gels.

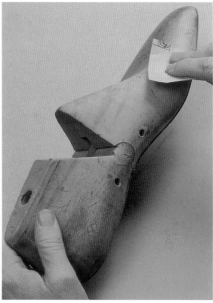

1 Vigorously sand the shoe last in the direction of the grain with medium sandpaper to remove all existing finish. After the finish has been eliminated, sand it with fine-grain sandpaper. (Heat from the woodburning tool may release noxious fumes if the finish is not completely eliminated, so pay careful attention to this step.) Brush away the dust. Enlarge the templates on page 74 to the size indicated. Use a ballpoint pen to trace the templates onto inter-facing, and cut out each of the motifs.

YOU WILL NEED

Adult-sized antique shoe last

Medium- and fine-grain sandpapers

Design templates (page 74)

Masking tape

Non-fusible interfacing

Graphite paper

Ballpoint pen

Sharp pencil (no. 2)

Eraser

Soft, lintfree cloth

Transparent blending gels: white, golden yellow, lemon yellow, light blue, French blue, lilac, orange, rouge, red, fuschia, pink, olive green, dark green

Satin acrylic varnish

Scissors

Woodburner with small, rounded point

¾-inch (1.9 cm) flat, white nylon or sable paintbrushes

Small, round, white nylon or sable paintbrush

2 Complete the rose in three stages. First, tape the rose stem and leaf at an angle across the toe of the shoe last. (Leave enough space for adding the rose bud later.) Slip graphite paper underneath. Retrace the lines with a ballpoint pen. Remove the design, and check the lines. Darken lines that are unclear with a pencil. Transfer the design for the rosebud separately, placing it atop the stem, then add the rose leaf. Transfer the remaining motifs separately and repeat them—the fan, the bird, the butterfly, and ribbons—around the body of the last as you like.

4 Use transparent blending gels and the small paintbrush to color the designs. (For the fan we used French blue, the small roses on it are pink with leaf green leaves, and the ribbon is lilac.) Paint small areas one at a time, working with a single color.

5 Use a cloth to blot off the excess color, then gently rub until the paint has a transparent look. If needed, dampen the rag with water and rub some more. Any small mistakes can be easily erased at this point.

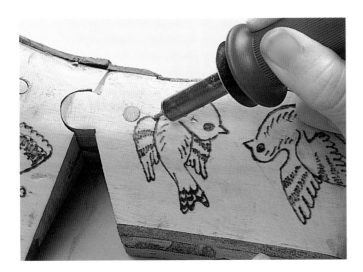

3 Insert a small, rounded point, and heat the woodburner. Outline all of the designs. If you want to fill in spaces with more of the designs, keep adding them. When finished, use the eraser to remove all pencil and graphite marks.

6 Paint the rest of the designs using colors of your choice. When the paint is dry, paint a coat of varnish on the whole piece. After the varnish dries, sand the piece lightly. Apply another coat of varnish.

TIP To give this piece a lustrous finish, apply a coat of automobile paste wax instead of varnish. Follow the instructions on the can, and rub the surface until it takes on a warm, even shine.

Cat's Delight Gourd

Your cat will love this tribute to his gastronomical fantasy in which he finds a fish as large as himself! After bleaching the outside of your gourd, it makes an interesting surface to burn. Gourds have a slightly different texture than wood, and their color provides an ideal background for burned designs.

TIP Instead of non-fusible interfacing, you can use a clothes softening dryer sheet as a substitute. Wash it thoroughly to remove the chemicals, then press it dry and smooth it with a warm iron. Trace your design lightly with a ballpoint pen to prevent fraying.

TIP As you're burning the gourd, its skin will leave deposits on the point of the woodburner, making it difficult to move the point after a few minutes of burning. Keep a piece of medium sandpaper nearby, and occasionally wipe the hot points across it to clean them.

3 Use a hatching pattern, or other design of your choice, to fill in the body of the cat. Whatever pattern you choose should be simple.

1 Dry and clean the gourd as described on page 65. Wrap the cloth measuring tape around the fattest part of the gourd. Using it as a guide, make six evenly-spaced pencil marks around the periphery of the gourd. These marks will be used as a guide for positioning the centers of the fish and cat designs. Enlarge the templates on page 72 to the size indicated. Use the ballpoint pen to trace the cat and fish templates onto the non-fusible interfacing. Cut them apart, and center the cat on one of the pencil marks. Tape the design in place, and slip graphite paper underneath. Trace the design with a ballpoint pen. After removing the design, darken any lines that are too light. Repeat this process for tracing the fish, and alternate a cat and a fish design around the span of the gourd. (If your gourd will only accommodate four designs, that's fine.) While turning it slowly, pencil two lines around the neck of the gourd that will form a solid band. Using our piece as a springboard for your own ideas, add other bands around the top, which you can fill in with patterns and textured lines later.

4 Change to a shading point, and use it to create a dark band on the neck of the gourd. Move the flat area of the point slowly and evenly over the surface, skimming back and forth as you go.

Burn the darkest areas at the top of the gourd with the same point. Switch the woodburner to a large, rounded point, and burn designs of your choice between the bands. Erase all pencil and transfer lines. Wipe away any eraser crumbs.

2 Insert the large, rounded point, and heat the wood-burner. Outline the fish and cat designs, and detail the cats' faces and the fishes' gills, eyes, and mouths. Move slowly with the burner to create distinct lines.

5 Coat all surfaces of the gourd with at least two layers of acrylic varnish. You may wish to use matte on the design portion of the gourd, and satin on the top and bottom parts.

Gourd Lamp

A smiling sun will greet you every time you turn on this cheerful lamp made from a gourd. After burning the design on both the gourd and the shade, use fabric dyes to color the simple shapes that make up this bold luminary.

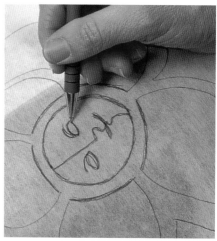

1 Enlarge the template on page 75 to the size indicated. Use the ballpoint pen to trace the design template onto non-fusible interfacing. Tape the design in place on the gourd, slip graphite paper underneath it, and trace it onto the gourd by drawing over the lines of the interfacing with the ballpoint pen. Remove the template, and darken the lines of the design with the pencil.

YOU WILL NEED

Large, round kettle gourd, about 12-14 inches (30 x 35 cm) tall, with flat bottom	Sharp pencil (no. 2)	Lamp shade kit with kraft paper cover
	Eraser	Matte or satin acrylic varnish
Cloth measuring tape	Fabric dyes: light yellow, dark yellow, orange, and red	Wood glue or white craft glue
Design templates (page 75)		Scissors
Ballpoint pen	Matte or satin acrylic varnish	Woodburner with large, rounded point
Non-fusible interfacing	Kit for converting a basket to a lamp (see supplier's list on page 79, or check your local craft store)	¾-inch and ½-inch (1.9 and 1.3 cm) flat, white nylon paintbrushes
Masking tape		Small, round, white nylon paintbrush
Graphite paper	Sturdy wooden slat, about 2 x 6 x ¼-inch (5 x 15 x .6 cm) thick	Craft knife with several sharp blades
		Small handsaw (optional)

2 Insert the large, rounded point, and heat the woodburner. Outline the lines of the design slowly, and go back over them if necessary. Erase all pencil and transfer lines after you've finished burning the design. Use the small, round and

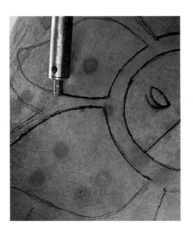

small, flat paintbrushes to brush a generous coat of the lightest yellow fabric dye over the face of the sun, staying within the lines of the design.

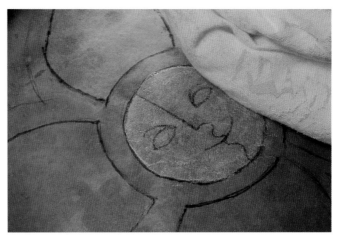

3 Blot the dye with a clean cloth so the gourd's texture can be seen through the paint. (The color will probably look slightly mottled after you do this, adding texture to the design.) Next, follow the same procedure to add orange dye to the "rays" that touch the circle. Last, add red dye to the outermost "rays." After the dyes have dried thoroughly, coat all surfaces of the gourd with at least two layers of acrylic varnish.

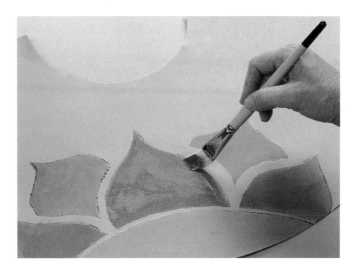

4 Transfer the shade pattern from the template to tracing paper. Trace it onto the shade. Burn the outlines of the pattern with the large, rounded point. Paint the design on the shade with the ½-inch (1.3 cm) flat paintbrush, using the dyes and the same procedure that you did with the gourd.

CLEANING AND CUTTING THE GOURD

Before beginning this project, you'll need to clean and dry the gourd, then cut the neck off so that a lamp fixture can be added later. To do this, fill a small plastic tub or other container with a solution of one cup (240 mL) of bleach and about a gallon (3.8 L) of water. Grab an old white towel, your gourd, and the tub containing bleach solution. Take them all outside on a sunny day. Dip the towel in the bleach solution, wrap the gourd in it, and place it in a sunny spot. (Use rubber gloves when doing this if you have sensitive hands.) The heat of the sun will steam the side of the gourd that is exposed to the heat. Reposition the gourd every 15 minutes or so until you've bleached the gourd on all sides. Scrub any remaining mold off with a fingernail brush or bristle brush. Dry the gourd thoroughly. Then set the gourd upright on a level surface, and place a pencil at the point where you want to cut off the neck. (Make certain that the hole that's left once you remove the neck will span several inches, allowing enough room to add the lamp fixture.) Turn the gourd slowly, and make a mark that is level around the circumference of the gourd. First use a craft knife to gouge a line on top of your penciled line. Use this line as a guide, and carefully saw the neck of the gourd off with the knife or a small saw, being careful not to cut in the direction of your fingers.

7 Push the cord down into the gourd, and pull the plug end out of the small hole you've cut to accommodate it. Pick up the slat in preparation for clipping the light bulb holder to it.

5 To assemble the lamp, first measure the size of the plug, and cut a hole in the back side of the gourd with a craft knife to accommodate the plug.

8 Pull the lamp cord through the gourd. Put the slat into the slots on the neck, and clip the light to it. If the gourd doesn't balance well, clip the light to the other side of the slat, and see if that position is better. After you decide on the best position for the light, affix the slat in its slots with wood glue.

6 Use a craft knife or small handsaw to cut a short piece of wooden slat that will reach across the top of the open neck. Lay the slat across the neck. Use a pencil to mark the underside of the slat where it intersects the top of the gourd on both sides. Use these marks as a guide for trimming the slat so that it sits flush with the sides of the opening on the top of the gourd. Next, look down on the top of the slat and mark its position on the top of the neck with pencil lines. Use these lines as a guide to carve a slot on each side that is the width and the depth of the slat. After doing this, the slat should lie level in the slots. Remove the slat, varnish it, and set it aside for later. Varnish the top edge of the gourd, the hole in the gourd, and all sides of the wooden slat to avoid warping. Allow the varnish to dry.

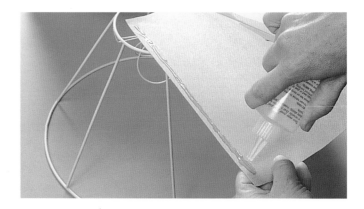

9 To assemble the shade after it's been decorated, squeeze a line of glue along the inside edge. Wrap the paper shade around the wire frame, overlap the edges, and hold it in place for about a minute until the glue has begun to set. Allow it to dry thoroughly before placing it on the wire frame.

Colorful Fruit Tray

Voluptuous fruit fills the bottom of this double-handled tray, which is edged with gold. By using wax-based colored pencils, you can create the realistic dimension found on this piece. This project is a great way to learn about layering, highlighting, and shading.

Small wooden tray, 10 x 3 x 9 inches (25 x 7.5 x 22.5 cm)	Wax-based oil pencils: magenta, crimson red, carmine red, white, vermillion, orange, canary yellow, burnt ochre, yellow orange, spring green, parrot green, dark green, mulberry, violet, dark purple, lavender
Fine-grain sandpaper	
Design template (page 73)	Soft, lintfree cloth
Masking tape	Gold acrylic paint
Graphite paper	Satin acrylic varnish
Sharp pencil (no. 2)	Woodburner with large, rounded point
Eraser	Scissors
Cotton swabs	¾-inch (1/9 cm) flat, white nylon paintbrush

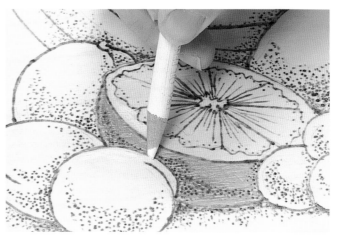

1 Sand the tray in the direction of the grain, and round off sharp edges. Brush away the dust. Apply strips of masking tape along the sides of the tray to prevent unwanted burn marks later. Enlarge the template on page 73 to the size indicated. Trace the design template onto tracing paper or other thin paper. Tape the design in the center of the tray, and slip graphite paper underneath before tracing it with a pencil. Remove the design and graphite paper, then darken the lines of the design with pencil as needed.

3 Color the fruit with the colored pencils, layering two or three colors in each fruit, leaf, or stem to increase the realism and to add depth to the design. Begin by placing highlights on each fruit, using white or the palest color.

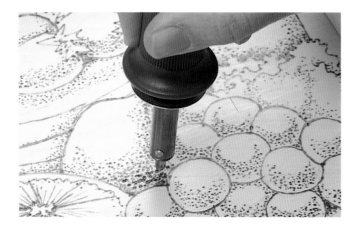

2 Insert the large, rounded point, and heat the woodburner. Burn the design's outlines at about half the pace of writing with a pen. Cover areas of shading on and between the fruit with stippling, or small dots. Use the gray end of the eraser to remove all pencil and graphite marks. Finish cleaning the surface with the white end of the eraser. Wipe off any eraser crumbs.

4 After highlighting the fruits with white, fill in the outlines of each fruit with color. Avoid the white areas that you want to leave highlighted.

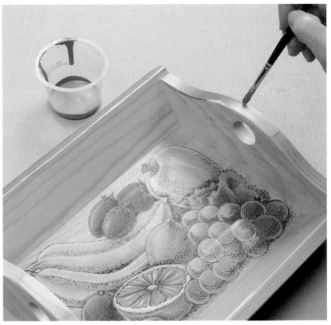

5 Blend the colors with a cotton swab as you work. Brush or blow away any flakes of wax that may accumulate while working. If you make a mistake with colored pencil, remember that it can usually be erased or sanded away.

7 To give the tray a finished look, paint the edges and the outside with gold acrylic paint. After the paint dries, paint the entire tray, inside and out, with a coat of acrylic varnish. Lightly sand it before applying the second coat of varnish.

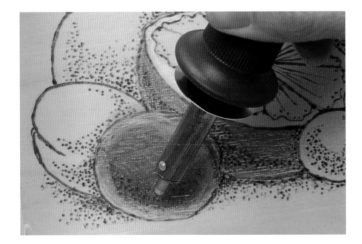

6 Reburn any lines that are unclear on top of the colored pencil work. While doing this, wipe the burner's point often on sandpaper to clean it. After you've finished coloring and burning the design, remove the masking tape.

TEMPLATES

ENLARGE ALL DESIGNS 200%,
OR DOUBLE THEIR SIZE.

Variations
(page 53)

Drapery Rod and Finials
(page 51)

Nana's Cherry Box
(page 36)

Lotus Flower Plate
(page 58)

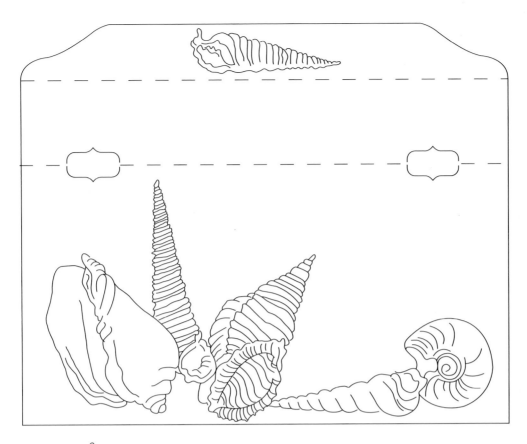

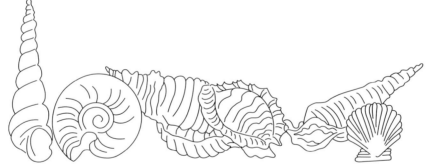

Seaside Bath Accessory
(page 54)

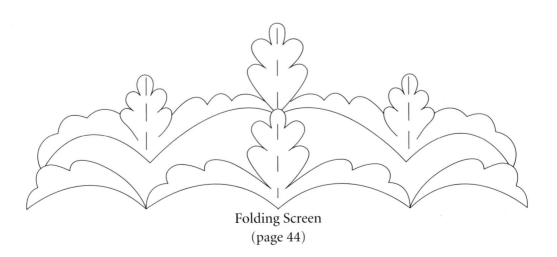

Folding Screen
(page 44)

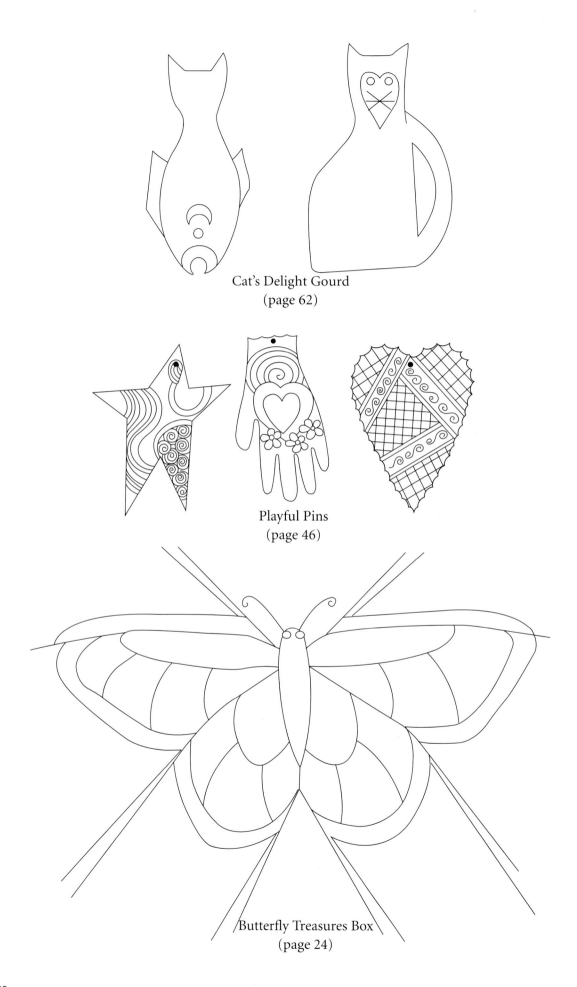

Cat's Delight Gourd
(page 62)

Playful Pins
(page 46)

Butterfly Treasures Box
(page 24)

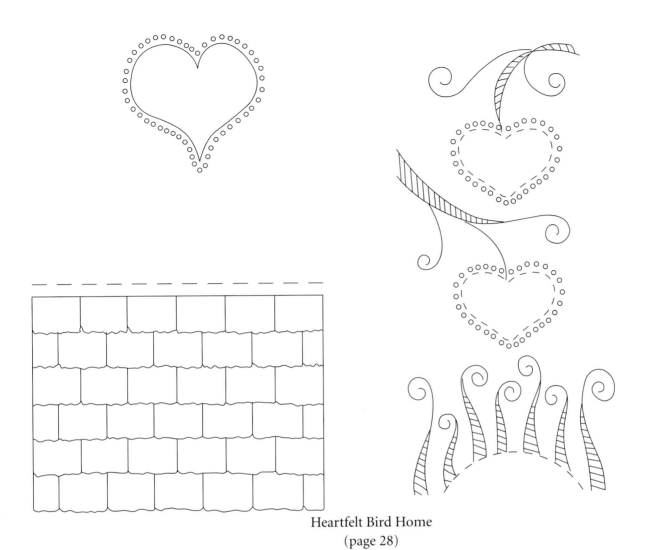

Heartfelt Bird Home
(page 28)

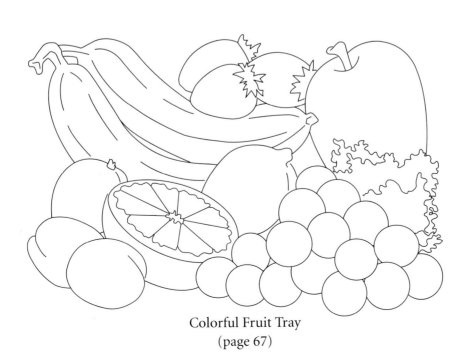

Colorful Fruit Tray
(page 67)

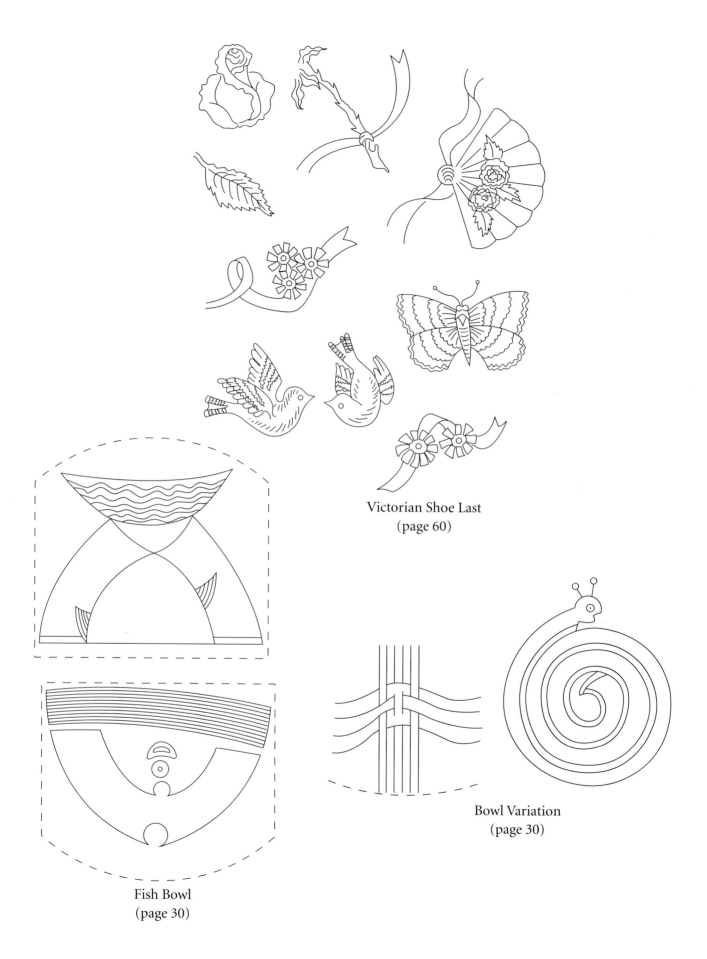

Victorian Shoe Last
(page 60)

Fish Bowl
(page 30)

Bowl Variation
(page 30)

Gourd Lamp
(page 54)

Ladder-back Chair
(page 42)

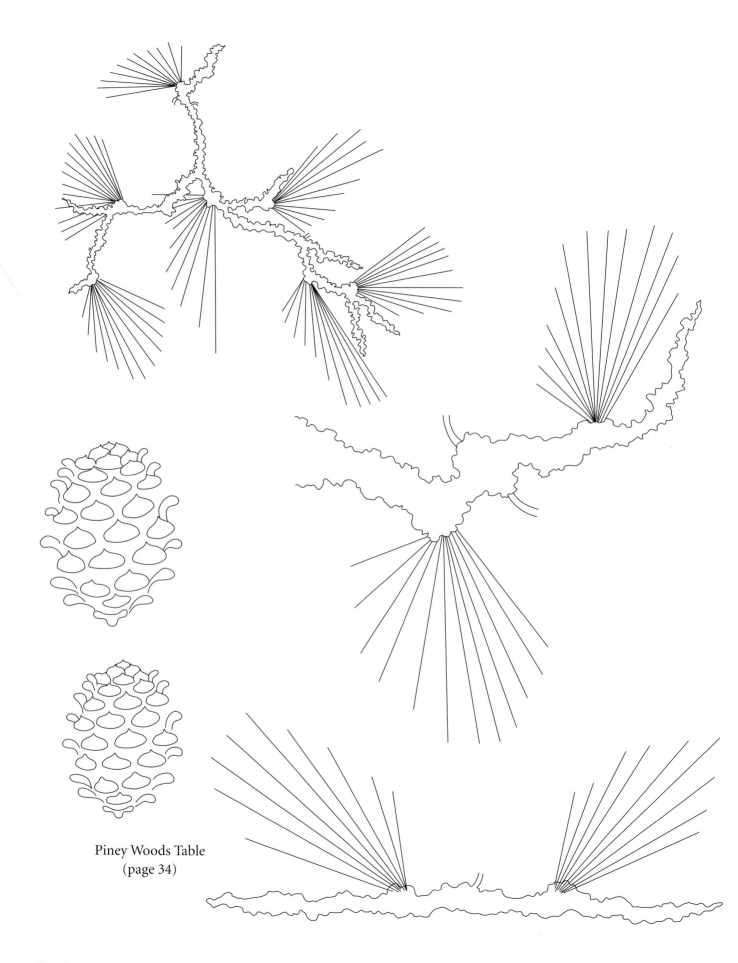

Piney Woods Table
(page 34)

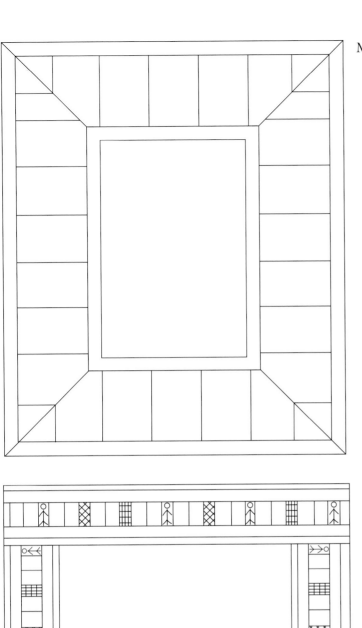

Memory Album
(page 38)

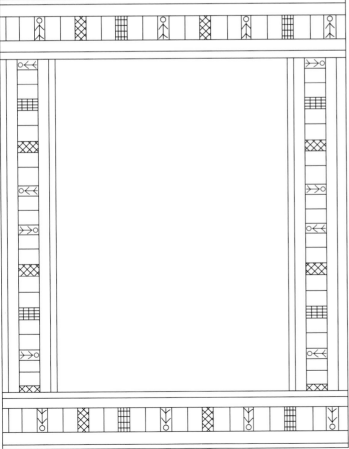

Patterned Frame
(page 40)

Holiday Ornaments
(page 26)

African Safari Planter Box
(page 32)

SUPPLIERS

UNFINISHED WOOD, WOODBURNERS AND POINTS, AND COLORED PENCILS:

Walnut Hollow
1409 State Road 23
Dodgeville, Wisconsin 53533-2112
1-800-395-5995
Mail order catalog available

TRANSPARENT BLENDING GELS, FABRIC PAINTS, GEL WOOD STAINS, FAUX GLAZEBASE, AND ACRYLIC PAINTS:

Delta Technical Coatings, Inc.
2550 Pellissier Boulevard
Whittier, California 90601
1-800-423-4135
web site: http:/www.deltacrafts.com
Available in craft, hobby, and
discount stores everywhere

PAINTBRUSHES:

Loew-Cornell Inc.
563 Chestnut Avenue
Teaneck, New Jersey 07666-2490
(201) 836-7070
loewcornel@aol.com
Available in art, craft, office supply, and
discount stores everywhere

TRANSPARENT RULERS:

The C-Thru Ruler Co.
6 Britton Drive
Bloomfield, Connecticut 06002-3602
(860) 243-0303
ccthru@aol.com
Available in art, craft, sewing, and
office supply stores everywhere

LAMP KIT AND LAMPSHADE KIT:

Kiti
A Division of Woodstock Wireworks, Inc.
300 North Seminary Ave.
Woodstock, Illinois 60098
1-800-435-8083
kitiinc@aol.com
Available at hobby, craft, fabric and
discount stores everywhere

WOODEN ANTIQUE SHOE LAST:

Artifacts, Inc.
P.O. Box 3399
Palestine, Texas 75802-3399
(903) 729-4178
artifacts@e-tex.com
Mail order catalog available

CONTRIBUTING GALLERY DESIGNERS

Bunny DeLorie lives in Goleta, California where she operates her design business, Fe Fi Faux Finish.™ She is the Co-Host of Your Home Studio on TNN cable television. She is also a designer and demonstrator for QVC Network, Home and Garden Television (HGTV), and The Discovery Channel.

David A. Gregory lives in Eldrid, New York where he works as a full-time machinist. Several years ago he discovered woodburning as a hobby to fill his time in the cold winter months when he couldn't hunt or fish. Now he proudly produces gifts for all of his relatives.

Dyan Mai Peterson is a nationally known gourd artist and teacher. She enjoys experimenting with any size or shape of gourd that she can find or grow, to produce decorative bowls, jewelry, and dolls. Her studio and home are located in Asheville, North Carolina.

Vicki Schreiner lives in Springfield, Missouri, and splits her time between designing, teaching, and demonstrating woodburning techniques that involve new ways of using color. She is also the author of *Creative Woodburning Children's Decor* and *Creative Woodburning Folkart*, both published by Walnut Hollow. Her newest book, entitled *Easy Woodburning with Color*, was published by Grace Publications.

Dennis and Vivian Williams live in Asheville, North Carolina. Dennis has designed furniture for over 20 years, emphasizing rustic furniture for the past three years. His work is represented by Grovewood Gallery in Asheville. Vivian enjoys experimenting with a variety of crafts.

ACKNOWLEDGMENTS

Special thanks and appreciation to Dave Ladd, Chris Wallace, and all the other friendly people of Walnut Hollow for their continuing support of designers and wood-burning as an art form. Walnut Hollow provided most of the wood pieces found in the project section of this book, as well as the wood-burners and colored pencils.

Thanks to Deborah Morgenthal and Carol Taylor of Lark Books for recognizing that woodburning is an artful craft that can be done by anyone, and for giving me the opportunity to write this book. Thanks to Evan Bracken for the beautifully styled photography. Thanks also to Thom Gaines and Kathy Holmes for the handsome layout. A designer can create outstanding pieces, but sensitively created and placed photographs bring them to life.

Thanks to Debra Garner, Barbara Carson, and Barbie Vasek at Delta for their immediate response to repeated requests for more stain and varnishes as the projects multiplied. Quality always shows. Thanks also to Enviro Depot in Asheville, North Carolina, for providing props for the photo shoot.

The biggest thanks goes to Katherine Duncan, the best editor in the world, for her inspiration, energy, exper-tise, unflagging sense of humor, and most of all friendship. Without all of those things, this book would never have been written.

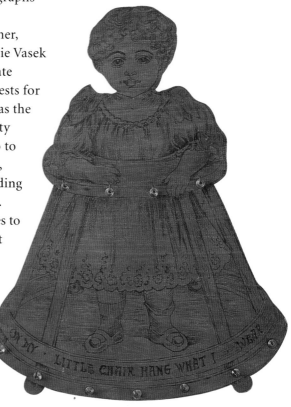

INDEX